"Fr. Michael Giesler's b[...] [...] *ue jorce*! He sets forth a compelling account of the profound social implications of the Paschal Mystery. *How Christ Saves Souls—with Us: The Mystery of Co-Redemption* draws out the theological inferences that cascade from the claim situated at the heart of the Catholic faith, namely, that God chooses to involve humanity in his redemptive plan. Twentieth century Catholic theology was particularly attuned to the doctrine of redemptive suffering. Fr. Giesler offers a theological exclamation mark to this truth, which was lived out by heroic saints such as Maximilian Kolbe, Teresa of the Cross, Padre Pio, and Teresa of Calcutta and was emphasized in the teaching of saintly popes such as Pius X, Pius XI, and John Paul II. In this volume the sacramental, pastoral, and theological reverberations of the doctrine of the communion of saints sound with clarity and beauty."

—Dr. Gerald Boersma,
Ave Maria University

"Like St. Paul, we make up what is lacking in Our Lord's suffering for the sake of others (Colossians 1:24). This is the mystery of redemptive suffering, and it is the great dignity given to Christians. Not only do we imitate Jesus. We participate in his saving work. No book tells this truth as clearly and practically as Fr. Giesler's . . . This little volume will change the way you look at life's hardships. In doing so, it will change your life—and then you will change the lives of countless others."

—Mike Aquilina,
Award-winning author of more than fifty books
on Catholic history, doctrine, and devotion

HOW CHRIST
Saves Souls—with Us

HOW CHRIST
Saves Souls—with Us

THE MYSTERY OF CO-REDEMPTION

FR. MICHAEL GIESLER
Foreword by Scott Hahn

Steubenville, Ohio
www.emmausroad.org

Emmaus Road Publishing
1468 Parkview Circle
Steubenville, Ohio 43952

Library of Congress Control Number 2022930559
ISBN 978-1-64585-199-8 (paperback)
978-1-64585-200-1 (ebook)

Cover design by Allison Merrick
Layout by Joseph Antoniello and Allison Merrick
Cover image: Giovanni Lanfranco, *The Miracle of the Loaves and Fishes* (1624-1625), National Gallery of Ireland.

This book is dedicated to the Holy Spirit,
who likes to remain unseen but who works deeply
in the soul of every human person.
I pray that the reader may experience His transforming
power in each chapter of this little book.

Table of Contents

Foreword by Scott Hahn   xi

Preface   xv

Theological Introduction   xix

Christ the Redeemer   1

The Church and the Communion of Saints   13

Faith   35

Prayer   49

Sanctifying Work   59

Matrimony as Co-Redemption   69

Giving Witness   83

Co-Redemptive Friendship   95

The Holy Mass: Center of Our Redemption on Earth   107

The Slavery of Sin   121

The Overwhelming Power of Charity   133

Making Atonement: Redemptive Sacrifice   143

Sanctifying Illness and Suffering   155

Easter Joy   165

Mary Co-Redemptrix   175

Foreword

PRESBYTERIANS OF A CERTAIN DISPOSITION look back to the late nineteenth century and early twentieth century as a kind of golden age of American Calvinism. It was the time of the great "Princeton Theologians," chief of whom was B. B. Warfield.

When I was very young, I was a Presbyterian so disposed, and I first encountered the work of Warfield when I was in high school. I was especially fond of the five lectures he delivered as a kind of manifesto in 1914. They were later published in book form in *The Plan of Salvation*.

From Warfield I learned about *monergism*. Derived from the Greek words for "one" (*mono*) and "work" (*ergon*), the term was a neat summary of Calvinist Christianity. Salvation, Warfield proclaimed, was the work of God alone. God was sovereign and almighty, solely responsible for creation and redemption. All other religions, he argued, were "autosoteric"—that is, they taught some form of *self*-salvation. He was quite fond of Greek compounds.

Opposed to *monergism* was *synergism*, the notion that human beings had any role to play, any work to do, in the process of salvation. Warfield contended—and I concurred— that Roman Catholics were *autosoteric* and *synergistic*, and this made them the most dangerous sort of heretics.

I held to this fervently until I was undone by another Greek compound. This one was in Scripture. Reading St. Paul's First Letter to the Corinthians, I came upon this short sentence: "For we are God's fellow workers" (1 Cor 3:9). I had read it before, of course, but this time it startled me because it seemed irreconcilable with my beloved Warfield. Could we have anything at all to contribute to our salvation?

The English phrasing was troubling, and I was sure it must have been a problematic translation. So I looked it up in the original Greek—and that was even more troubling. "God's fellow workers" was an accurate rendering of *"Theou . . . synergoi."*

In case you haven't figured it out, *synergoi* is the very root of Warfield's bogeyman, *synergism*! Thus the Bible itself bore witness against this key tenet of Calvinism, and the sacred page had moved me another mile closer to the Catholic faith.

We are God's fellow workers. That is the point of this book; and it is a doctrine implicit in much of St. Paul and explicit not only in First Corinthians but also in his Letter to the Colossians: "Now I rejoice in my sufferings for your sake, and in my flesh I complete what is lacking in Christ's afflictions for the sake of his body, that is, the Church" (1:24). What could possibly be lacking in Jesus' perfect, once-for-all sacrifice of suffering? Nothing, right? Nothing, except what he willed to be lacking for our sake.

Like a good older brother, he let us share his work, so that we'd grow to be more like him.

This is the real "plan of salvation." Yes, God is all powerful. But he is also all good. And a good father is one who uses his power to make his children powerful. By sharing his power, God proves his power. Our cooperation manifests his fatherhood. He is not threatened by the works of his children. Indeed, they really belong to him. As our priests say to God in the preface of the Mass, "You are praised in the company of your saints and, in crowning their merits, you crown your own gifts."

This is the true meaning of the word "hierarchy." The word comes from yet another Greek compound, meaning "sacred order." In its original sense, hierarchy means an order in which the upper ranks reach down to the lower—*to empower them* and lift them up. St. Gregory the Great believed this, and that's why he lived his papacy as "servant of the servants of God." After the divine model, he "emptied himself, taking the form of a servant" (Phil 2:7). We would all do well to exercise our power in this way, in imitation of God.

Just to be clear: our part in redemption is *essentially* different from Christ's. Ours, in fact, would be impossible without his; and it is he who merited our capacity to merit. Nothing we do—nothing Mary does, and nothing the saints do—can add to what Christ has done or take anything away from his saving work. All we can hope to do is what he wishes us to do: to exemplify his salvation, to work with him, to be *synergoi*.

St. Augustine summed up the matter beautifully: "God who created you without you, will not save you without you" (St. Augustine, *Sermo* 169, 11, 13; cf. *CCC* 1847.) God wants all of us to be his fellow workers. Jesus said: "pray therefore the Lord of the harvest to send out laborers into his harvest" (Matt 9:38). Let us, who read this book, be the answer to that prayer.

That, I know, is the hope of the author. Father Michael Giesler is a great scholar of Scripture. He earned a doctorate, and he wrote his dissertation on the use of the Old

Testament by the authors of the New Testament. But he wears his learning lightly. He is also the author of helpful popular booklets on prayer—and a trilogy of novels about Christians in second-century Rome. He knows how to communicate obscure and difficult material in the language of non-scholars. He has been my friend and respected colleague for four decades.

So take up and read, "and raise your heads, because your redemption is drawing near" (Luke 21:28), and by God's grace you have work to do.

Scott Hahn

Preface

WE HAVE ALL HEARD THE EXPRESSION "mind your own business." Perhaps we ourselves have said it to an individual who is being overly curious about something in our lives, or asking something very personal. In these cases, it makes sense. But at other times it can be a kind of escape mechanism when someone sincerely wants to help us and we turn him or her away. It can be the rude answer of a person who doesn't really want to think about his or her life in a serious way, or to change what needs to be changed.

Jesus Christ minded His business, and *our* business, when He came to this world. He did not want to live as an isolated deity in the sky who really doesn't care about the human race He created. He took the tremendous risk of coming to this world, becoming like us in everything but sin—and eventually dying for us. In other words, He made a *real commitment* to us. As St. Paul writes to an early Christian community, Jesus "did not count equality with God a thing to be grasped, but emptied himself, taking the form of a servant, being born in the likeness of men" (Phil 2:6–7).

If we are to find real fulfillment and happiness in our life, we, too, must learn to forget about ourselves and give ourselves truly to God and to others. This is the constant message of the Gospel, of the early Christians, of all the saints throughout the ages, and most recently of Popes John Paul II and Benedict XVI. "Real love is demanding," the former once said to a large group of young people. "I would fail in my mission if I did not clearly tell you so. . . . Love demands effort and a personal commitment to the will of God. It means discipline and sacrifice, but it also means joy and human fulfillment."[1]

Today there are many ways to escape the challenge of Christ and His love. We can immerse ourselves in business concerns, hobbies, or entertainment and give very little attention to God or to others. We can distract ourselves in a technological world of smartphones, Facebook, and tweets; we could even run the risk of rarely looking a fellow human being in the eye or trying to get to know him or her personally. We can avoid taking a stand on anything—including the dignity of human life and the existence of right and wrong—and in doing so we can even be praised for being "up-to-date and informed," or "intellectually progressive and cool." We can even be noncommittal about the permanence of marriage, the existence of God, and the need for a Church—and find acceptance and support from many voices in the modern media, including a multitude of contemporary authors and agnostic college professors.

But ultimately, ours would be a sad and meaningless life. No truth. No love. No goals. No adventure. In the end, our existence would be extremely *boring*, the expression used by Pope Francis to challenge people at the 2016 World Youth Day in Poland. In such a world, we would suffocate since we have nothing to live for, or to die for. In the words of Shakespeare's famous tragedy, we would experience exactly what

[1] Pope St. John Paul II, "Homily of His Holiness John Paul II" (Apostolic Journey to the United States, Boston, October 1, 1979), §6, https://www.vatican.va/content/john-paul-ii/en/homilies/1979/documents/hf_jp-ii_hom_19791001_usa-boston.html.

Macbeth experienced after years of selfishness, violence, and greed: "[Life]/ is a tale told by an idiot, full of sound and fury, signifying nothing."[2]

Not so if we believe in Jesus Christ and His Church. For He said, "I am the way, the truth, and the life" (John 14:6), and "He who believes in me, though he die, yet shall he live, and whoever lives and believes in me shall never die" (John 11:25–26). If we have faith in Him and His Church, which is His Bride in heaven and on earth, we will see the way clearly. We will discover that there *is* a truth worth knowing, living, and even dying for. There *is* a plan and a love that give meaning to our life, and they lead us to forget about ourselves and to think of others. Life then becomes for us just the opposite of Macbeth's tragic line: it becomes *a tale told by Jesus Christ, full of love and adventure, signifying everything.*

Such is the story of redemption and co-redemption. Such was the message of St. John to those early followers of Christ who were trying to change the world for Christ, one person at a time, one family at a time. They were indeed like the light in a very dark, pagan world—a world largely based on greed and lust. Yet somehow Christ and His followers prevailed and gradually changed people's attitudes toward life, family, work, even entertainment. They realized that they were His chosen ones, and that He would never abandon them. In union with Him they truly redeemed the world, though for many it cost them their lives.

This book is to help you appreciate the mystery of redemption and co-redemption. Christ and His Church are

---

[2] William Shakespeare, *Macbeth*, 5.5.25–26.

still working in the world. Despite the action of the evil one, despite the ignorance and indifference of so many people (including Catholics), despite the hypocrisy and scandals that have hit the Church, Christ continues to work in history, and He continues to act through faithful men and women who will listen to His word, stand up for the truth, and spread His light and love to those around them. He also seeks men and women who do *not run away from the cross*, for it is through that cross that Jesus Christ continues to save every soul on earth.

In this book you will find the theological and biblical principles that you need to become a true co-redeemer. I hope you enjoy it, and that you are able to apply them to your daily life in the middle of society.

Theological Introduction

As Christians, we believe that the Blessed Trinity, from all eternity, willed to save us from sin and bring us into the joy of their own life. All three Persons accomplished our redemption, working together as one, as they did in the miracle of creation. Both creation and redemption are called *ad extra* actions of the Trinity by Catholic theologians; that is, they take place outside of the intimate life of knowledge and love between the three Persons, though all three Persons will these actions and are involved in them. More specifically, we can say that God the Father, in His providential plan for mankind, sent God the Son to save us from sin and bring us to everlasting life, and God the Holy Spirit sanctifies each one of us with His love and guides the Church until the end of time.

Yet it was only one of the Persons, God the Son, who actually became a human being like us. It was God the Son, Jesus Christ, who completely reconciled us with the other two Persons of the Trinity by His daily life, by His preaching and miracles, and above all by His painful death and glorious Resurrection. He is the New Adam who founded the new human race in His work, prayer, and sacrifice. He conquered Satan and the slavery of sin, and opened the way to heaven for all mankind, which is eternal life and everlasting happiness.

But we also believe that Christ chose to use men and women on this earth who freely unite themselves with Him and offer their work, prayer, and sufferings for others. This has been called the mystery of *co-redemption*, that is, the free participation of Christ's followers in the redemption of their fellow men and women.

But we need to understand the term co-redemption properly. Christ's disciples are not "equal" participants to Christ in redeeming the world but only work *with* Him in this task. (The prefix "co" in co-redemption is meant in the sense of accompanying, not of being equal.) No number of men or women, no matter how virtuous and sacrificial they may be, could make atonement for even one small sin, let alone redeem mankind. Therefore, a person does not co-redeem in the sense of someone who is co-author of a book, or co-pilot of an airplane.

All the grace and power of redemption must come from Christ, for He is the only one who really *merits* our redemption, as a divine Person in unity with the Father and the Holy Spirit. In Catholic Theology this is called merit *de condigno*, that is, a merit that is owed out of strict justice to the person meriting. Christ merited our salvation out of strict justice because of the dignity of His divine Person, and the infinite effect of His sacrifice, capable of satisfying God Himself since Christ Himself is God's Son. Our meriting of grace for others is called merit *de congruo*, that is, we can merit for others because God mercifully sees fit to grant us grace because of our good action, not because we strictly deserve it. Mary Mother of Jesus is the greatest example of *de congruo* merit,[1] and this could be extended

---

[1] For more on Mary as Mediatrix of Graces for mankind, see Pope St. Pius X, Encyclical Letter on the Immaculate Conception *Ad Diem Illum Laetissimum* (February 2, 1904). See also Pope Benedict XV, Apostolic Letter *Inter Soldalica*, Acta Apostolicae Sedis (AAS) 10 (March 22,

to all the faithful who perform good works with and for Christ. This *de congruo* merit could be applied to a soul in purgatory, to a colleague who's struggling against a grave sin, or even to people we don't know personally but whom we can help spiritually.

Co-redemption is indeed a great mystery since it has to do with God's infinite and profound plan of salvation for every human soul. In a way beyond our understanding, we can obtain grace for others by drawing from Christ's infinite love and merits. And He has freely chosen to manifest his redeeming power within us, which shows His divine greatness. This power flows from our *divine filiation*, by which we are made children of God and share in God's own inner life and are therefore pleasing to Him. It also flows from the fact that we are called to be other Christs: in the expression of St. Paul, to have Christ Himself living within us (Eph 3:17; Gal 2:20). His life actually begins in us through the grace of Baptism, when we are configured to Him, Christ the Redeemer, and receive His threefold mission and power: to teach, to sanctify, and to govern in His name.

We shall see later in this book how God's grace activates each of these three powers in our lives and interactions with others, thus making us *co-redeemers* and sharers in Christ's redemptive action in the world.

Co-redemption works in a particular way through the communion of saints. The saints in heaven and on earth have a privileged place for co-redemption since they are closest to the Source of all grace because of their prayerful and holy

---

1918): 181; and Pope St. John Paul II, Apostolic Letter on the Christian Meaning of Human Suffering *Salvifici Doloris* (February 11, 1984), §25.

lives. As members of the Church, Christ's Mystical Body on earth, we, too, can win many graces for ourselves and others if our souls are pleasing to God.

Theologically speaking, co-redemption is the result of our cooperation with an actual grace, or a transient help given by God to a soul in order to bring about a redemptive effect. It requires three conditions to be effective: the co-redeemer must normally be in the state of sanctifying grace (and therefore pleasing to God); his or her action must in itself be good and done with the right intention; and he or she must *freely* perform it. If these conditions are fulfilled, we can speak of a truly co-redemptive action. St. Paul alludes to this kind of action in his own life in his famous text to the Colossians: "Now I rejoice in my sufferings for your sake, and in my flesh I complete what is lacking in Christ's afflictions for the sake of his body, that is, the Church" (Col 1:24). Of course, as we mentioned before, nothing can be lacking in Christ's sacrifice for our redemption; yet, the graces of that sacrifice need to be *applied* to the human race throughout the centuries. And Christ deigns to use His Apostles—and us—as the extension of His saving love to distribute those graces to other people through our own prayers and sufferings in union with His.

Co-redemptive acts can be of a general nature, such as the ordinary works of a good Christian throughout his life. This includes the daily prayer and good actions of any faithful follower of Christ. By trying to imitate Christ's life as closely as possible, he is already participating in redemption. Parents teaching their children the faith, workers doing honest ethical tasks each day, friends helping each other in big or small ways, all of these things can contribute to bringing Christ's kingdom to earth and therefore His redemption to all mankind. There need not be a specific or conscious intention to bring Christ to others in most of these ordinary actions, since we can assume that most people have at least a general or virtual intention to be a good Christian and to do what God wants.

However, more graces and merits can come if a person specifically activates his daily intention by means of frequent offerings or other prayers. These bring the person closer to Christ's own mind and heart, which will deliver more redemptive graces to the world. In other words, the closer a person is to Christ, the only Redeemer, the more he forgets himself and lets Christ act within him. Such practices as the morning offering, the frequent dedication of work during the day, and the offering of small or big sacrifices form the basis for more co-redemptive graces during the day. For instance, if children are complaining about a difficult task or situation, parents will at times say to them, "Offer it up"; often this is meant only to be a rebuke or an encouragement but, taken seriously, it can be something that brings grace to the family and to the world.

At times a very small action (word or deed), which a person may do without even realizing it, can be truly powerful and co-redemptive. It could be a chance event or remark, but the Holy Spirit will use it to produce a much greater effect, either at the present moment or at a later time. For example, if they have humility and gratitude, a son or daughter may well be able to say to their father or mother: "Do you remember when you said or did that thing? It really helped me . . ." The father or mother may not even remember it, but that word or action had a powerful effect on their son or daughter. The same could be true of remarks made or actions done by relatives, friends, or even chance acquaintances. Somehow God uses them, even if their words or actions were misdirected, or they appeared to be rude or insulting, to bring truth and conversion to those around them. Grace works in hidden and mysterious ways in people's lives.

Other actions can be specifically co-redemptive, as when a person through prayer and sacrifice, and at times with considerable suffering, offers himself for the spiritual good of others in union with Christ. By spiritual good I mean that which pertains to another's justification and eternal salvation, or for a great work of sanctification for others. The history of the Church is filled with co-redemptive acts, which we will see throughout this book: the daily witness of the early Christians in the middle of pagan society to a life of joy, friendship, and service; their affection and care, at the risk of their own lives, to non-Christian families suffering from the plague; the heroic missionaries, who over the centuries have spread the faith throughout the world, many of whom died as martyrs; the prayer and sacrifice of countless Christians for the conversion of their families and friends.

In this regard we can remember those years of constant petition, mixed with tears, that St. Monica offered for the conversion of her son Augustine, or, for that matter, of the constant prayer and sacrifice of contemporary parents for the conversion of their straying children. The persevering prayer and sacrifice of a friend for his friend, to bring him back to the sacraments of the Church for instance, is a truly co-redemptive act. The courageous work of people in this country who want to convert minds and hearts in order to protect innocent human life and authentic marriage can also be truly co-redemptive, as long as such people have goals beyond mere political or legislative programs.

Co-redemptive actions often combine with great works of sanctification throughout history. I think of all those people who pray for priests doing exorcisms in order to cast out the evil one from people's souls, or those who offer constant prayer during key events in world history, such as the saying of the Rosary during the famous Battle of Lepanto in 1571, when non-Christian forces threatened to overrun Europe. I also think of the graces that St. Josemaría Escrivá needed to begin Opus Dei back in the 1930s, when he searched for "souls of atonement" who would offer their sufferings for the work he was beginning for the Church and all peoples. Besides many others, there was one beggar woman who offered her sufferings for the young priest's intentions. Fr. Josemaría met her one day in Madrid and asked if she could offer her suffering for an intention of his. Later on, he saw her in a hospital where she was dying. When he offered to pray for her cure, she told him that it would not do any good. In her own words: "You told me to pray for something that would give great glory to God, and to give him everything I could. I offered him what I have, my life."[2] Although she never joined Opus Dei, nor even knew what it was, St. Josemaría always considered that, spiritually, she was the first woman member. After she went to heaven, the work of Opus Dei began to go forward more quickly.

Though it sounds ironic, the most powerful way to be a co-redeemer is to *forget that you are one*. We must concentrate simply on imitating Jesus Christ and working for the salvation of souls. When this happens, we can truly say

---

[2] John F. Coverdale, *Uncommon Faith: The Early Years of Opus Dei, 1928–1943* (New York: Scepter, 2002), 64.

that Christ is working with his salvific grace inside of us, and we are really *one with him* in our word or action that brings redeeming grace to others. As I said at the beginning of this section, the only Redeemer is Christ the Lord, as sent by the Father in the love of the Holy Spirit, and we have a completely dependent and subordinate role. We are indeed grateful that God allows us to share "in the action" of saving souls, so to speak, though we do not merit it.

Regarding this truth, Pope Francis in a homily on the Feast of Our Lady of Guadalupe said that Mary never presented herself as Co-Redemptrix, but that she considered herself simply to be a disciple of Christ and nothing more.[3] He repeated this idea at his General Audience of March 24, 2021, when he stated that Our Lady helps us "as a Mother, not as a goddess, not as a co-redeemer." He also warned against exaggerating Mary's role in redemption, because "love exaggerate[s]." Earlier in the audience, in speaking of Christ as the sole Mediator and Redeemer, he also stated that there are "no co-redeemers with Christ."[4]

We cannot think that the Holy Father here is denying the unique role of Mary in our redemption, which has been continually affirmed by the tradition and magisterium of the Church throughout the centuries, but is simply illustrating

---

[3]   Pope Francis, "Homily of His Holiness Pope Francis," (Feast of Our Lady of Guadalupe, Holy Mass for Latin America, Vatican Basilica, December 12, 2019), https://www.vatican.va/content/francesco/en/homilies/2019/documents/papa-francesco_20191212_omelia-guadalupe.html.

[4]   Pope Francis, "Catechesis on Prayer 27: Praying in Communion with Mary" (General Audience, Library of the Apostolic Palace, March 24, 2021), https://www.vatican.va/content/francesco/en/audiences/2021/documents/papa-francesco_20210324_udienza-generale.html.

its proper context and meaning in light of the doctrinal truth of Christ as the Sole Redeemer of mankind. Nor should we think that he is denying the reality of how Christ's faithful cooperate with him in redeeming others, which is also deeply rooted in Sacred Scripture and the Magisterium.[5]

Many modern saints, particularly St. Maximilian Kolbe (d. 1941), St. Teresa Benedicta of the Cross (d. 1942), St. Pio of Pietrelcina (d. 1968), St. Teresa of Calcutta (d. 1997), and Pope St. John Paul II (d. 2005), make reference to the reality of co-redemption and Mary as Co-Redemptrix in their reflections and writings. It formed part of the public Magisterium of St. Pius X, St. Pius XI, and St. John Paul II on repeated occasions. In composing this book, I am particularly indebted to the reflections of St. Josemaría Escrivá, who often uses the terms "co-redemption" and "co-redeemers" in his writings. His thought permeates the following pages—especially his insight that each of us must be another Christ, Christ Himself (*Ipse Christus*). For a powerful example of this, consider his commentary on the Eleventh Station of the Cross in his book *The Way of the Cross*. After he reflects on Christ nailed to the Cross, with His arms outstretched in forgiveness to the entire human race, he writes: "And we, our soul rent with sorrow, say to Jesus in all sincerity; I am yours and I give my whole self to you; gladly do I nail myself to the cross, ready to be in the crossroads of this world, a soul

---

[5] For an excellent treatment of Pope Francis' two statements and how to understand them properly, see Robert Fastiggi, "Pope Francis and Mary Co-Redemptrix," Where Peter Is, December 27, 2019, updated April 11, 2020, https://wherepeteris.com/pope-francis-and-mary-co-redemptrix/; and Fastiggi, "Observations on Pope Francis' 'March 24, 2021' Comments," *Ecce Mater Tua* 4 (June 12, 2021): 2–6.

dedicated to you, to your glory, to the work of Redemption, the co-redemption of the whole human race."[6]

As you reflect on the pages of this book and see the challenging prospects of co-redemption in your life and that of others, I recommend that you always keep in mind the example of Mary of Nazareth and of the greatest saints. They do the most good, including co-redemption, when they themselves disappear and allow Christ in His universal love to work through them.

[6] St. Josemaría Escrivá, *The Way of the Cross* (New York: Scepter Publishers, 2015), 92.

CHAPTER I

Christ the Redeemer

I REMEMBER THE STORY of a college junior who was invited to a Friday night party by his fraternity friends. He was a young man who believed in Christ and His message, and he had some concerns about what kind of party this would be. When he got there, things began alright but then took a turn for the worse when alcohol was brought in. Most of his friends were underage and many of the young women at the party were as well. Voices got louder, and people began to yell foul words and curses. He felt uncomfortable and so did his girlfriend, who was a practicing Catholic like himself. They looked at each other, and they each went to close friends in the crowd to invite them to leave. Only one girl decided to leave with them, and as they left, they said a prayer for everyone there. The wild party continued, ending with drunkenness and sex.

How can one look at this story? Is it redemption? If so, it seems to have failed. Is it co-redemption? That also seems to have failed because the party continued. But if you look at the suffering and brave action of the couple and their friend who left the scene, co-redemption really did occur. The truth is that in Himself and others, Christ continues to suffer and redeem throughout the centuries, not only at immoral parties, but in all human actions where there is a choice involved between good and evil.

One central principle of co-redemption is clear from the

above story: we cannot always expect to see immediate results from our prayers and actions. At times, it can appear that we're failing, but if we offer it generously to God, our effort will be fruitful.

Another point to note has to do with our body and how to respect it. If we are to be co-redeemers, we are to respect what God has given us, and help others to do the same. The bodies of those who believe in Christ are temples of the Holy Spirit and should not be violated. As St. Paul wrote almost two thousand years ago: "Do you not know that your body is a temple of the Holy Spirit within you, which you have from God? You are not your own; you were bought with a price. So glorify God in your body" (1 Cor 6:19–20). St. Paul is writing to the Corinthians to remind them of their great dignity and honor: they've been redeemed by Jesus Christ, and they must not fall back into their previous life-styles. Their bodies have been made holy, and they are now pleasing to God.

But what is this "price" that St. Paul talks about? It's an important point since it has to do with both redemption and co-redemption, the topic of our book. As a matter of fact, the word *redemptio* in Latin, from which we get our English word, is a good translation of *lutron* in Greek, and *kippur* in Hebrew—both of which mean a ransom, or the buying back of something. The greatest ransom or redemption in the Old Testament was the liberation of the Hebrews from Egypt, which God (Yahweh) performed through the plagues, the crossing of the Red Sea, and the destruction of the Egyptian armies in pursuit. This momentous event was remembered in a special and sacred way by the Jewish people in the great feast of the Passover every year.

We as Christians believe that Christ is the fulfillment of redemption, not only for the Jews but for all men. His life on earth, which culminated in His Crucifixion and Resurrection, was a continuous action of redeeming, or buying back, the human race from sin and the power of the devil. He led us from death to life—*eternal life*; He led us from sadness to joy—*eternal joy*; He led us from selfishness to love—*eternal love*.

As we said earlier, redemption, like creation, is really the work of all three divine Persons, Father, Son, and Holy Spirit. More specifically, we can say that it was God the Father who sent God the Son to redeem us, and both of them sent God the Holy Spirit to sanctify us. Each Person is therefore involved in loving us and saving us, though only the Second Person became a man, lived a human life, and died on the Cross.

Such is the real reason for the effectiveness of Christ's life and sacrifice: as an infinite Person, only He could give equal reparation to the two infinite Persons offended by sin, who are also God. Even if all the men and women who ever lived would allow themselves to be crucified in reparation for their sins, they could not atone for a single one. Only an infinite Person with a divine nature can truly make atonement to an infinite God.

At the same time, Christ is a human being like you and me, and therefore He can offer that reparation for us, who are the ones offending. He worked for a living, grew up in a family, experienced hunger, thirst, cold, pain, and sadness, just as you and I can, but in a more intense way. He was unlike us only in this: He was a divine Person who had a perfect human nature, and therefore He could never commit a sin. Yet, out of love for us, and to redeem us (to "buy us back"), He took upon Himself all of our sins, and paid the full price for them in His soul and flesh. In St. Paul's graphic, almost shocking words, "For our sake he made him to be sin, . . . so that in him we might become the righteousness of God" (2 Cor 5:21).

It is hard for us in our experience today to understand such a complete, even wild love. We might be willing to help a good friend move to another house or apartment, we might visit her if she's sick, we might loan her some money, or if she is a student even help her with a paper or essay due for a certain course—but to give our life for this person and, even more, to offer ourselves as a substitute for her punishment if she is guilty of a grave crime—this is truly extra-ordinary dedication. It directly contradicts the "me first" attitude that we often see around us.

The more we know about redemption, the more exciting it becomes. As we shall show later, Christ's redeeming work actually allows us to redeem the world *with Him*. We, too, are human beings who can feel hunger, pain, cold, and disappointment. By connecting all of these human experiences with Christ the Redeemer, we can truly be His eyes, arms, and hands in the world.

I recall hearing the story of a small German village that was bombed by the Allies at the end of World War II. There was a very beautiful Catholic church in the middle of the town, which was hit by a bomb that fell into the sanctuary near the altar. Miraculously, it did little damage, but it did blow the arms off of the figure of Christ crucified, an exquisite work of art that dated from many centuries before. After the war ended, the people of the village gathered to discuss what to do about the ruins of the town, and particularly about the Christ figure with no arms. Some wanted to reproduce a whole new figure, others simply wanted to restore the arms. But in the end, they decided to leave the figure as it was, and to put an inscription underneath the statue: *Sie sind meine Arme*; you are my arms.

Can there be a more moving description of what is meant by co-redemption?

We saw something similar in the opening story of this section, the story of the party without Christ. But through our care and friendship with others, we can spread His truth and love. Through our pain and suffering we can accompany Him on the Cross, which is the source of all redemption. And if we sin, we know that through His merciful love and His sacraments we are restored.

How Redemption Began

To begin to understand the mystery of redemption, we should take special note of the miracle of the Incarnation. This singular event took place in the womb of a young woman in Galilee a little more than two thousand years ago. At that moment, redemption truly began for us because the Second Person of the Blessed Trinity, the Son of God Himself, became a tiny being within His mother and began His human existence. From that instant forward, all human life would be transformed throughout the centuries—including the life of unborn children.

Jesus Christ, like His Mother, was conceived without sin, and thus began to free us from sin in Himself. By assuming our human nature, He elevated and gave redemptive value to the smallest things of life, including all our daily duties involving work and family. In everything that He does, precisely because of His Incarnation, He is transforming and saving us.

Catholic theologians call this Christ's "theandric operations"; that is, they are actions done by a divine Person with two distinct natures—human and divine. He is truly the God-man. For this reason, we can really say that it is Jesus the man who repairs a table in Nazareth, but it is also God repairing a table. We can really say that it is Jesus the man who weeps over people's ingratitude, but it is also God weeping over people's ingratitude. We can really say that it was Jesus the man who was scourged at the pillar, but it is also God who was scourged.

Through His actions as God and man, therefore, Christ literally *connects* heaven and earth in both the smallest things He does and in the greatest miracles He does, especially the Resurrection. From the moment of His conception, therefore, He was redeeming us. He was liberating us from sin and opening the door to a new and glorious life in God. He was truly making us part of His family and freeing us from all the negative consequences of original sin—pride, greed, lust, anger, and all the rest. Redemption began with Mary's acceptance of God's plan for her, announced by the angel Gabriel, and her conceiving of God's Son.

Since that moment, the human race has never been the same, nor will it ever be.

The Evangelists proclaim this joyful truth again and again. St. John in his famous prologue states that we are now children of God, "who were born, not of blood nor of the will of the flesh nor of the will of man, but of God" (John

1:13). This re-birth truly divinizes our existence and gives us a joy and freedom that the neither the world nor our fellow humans with all their works, dreams, and projects can give us. It is a kind of plenitude that is communicated to our bodies and souls, a grace that leads to everlasting life (see John 1:16). Christ's redemption gives complete fullness and meaning to human existence since it connects our existence with Himself and His own experience as the God-man.

And what is existence? No one knows for certain when or how the universe began. Many scientists today think there was a primal explosion at some point, with the production of hydrogen and other elements, which then expanded. (We might add, a little mischievously for our atheist friends, that if there was a *Big Bang*, there must have been a *Big Banger*). However it all began, St. Paul states that even before creation God knew and loved each one of us who would live on this tiny planet earth; for He chose us to live in His Son before the foundation of time (see Eph 1:4). We are truly made alive in Christ, and because of this universal plan of redemption we are now citizens of heaven, and we look to the new heaven and the new earth at the end of time, which will be the fullness of God's presence among us (see Rev 21:1–4). Such is the power and sweep of God's plan for each one of us. "Behold, I make all things new" (Rev 21:5), the Savior says, who is the conquering King of heaven and earth.

The Blood of the Redeemer

But the story of redemption, and co-redemption, goes even deeper.

Such a liberation from sin and death, and such a great

victory, came at a great price. And it continues to come at that same price—namely, the blood of the King, who is the Lamb of God. Just as the Jews offered a lamb in sacrifice at the first Passover Meal in Egypt, Christ offered Himself on the Cross for all of us. He is both the priest of our redemption and its victim. This was predicted in the Old Testament in the mysterious verses of Isaiah: "He was despised and rejected by men; a man of sorrows, and acquainted with grief; and as one from whom men hide their faces he was despised, and we esteemed him not" (Isa 53:3). The cost of redemption, therefore, was rejection and scorn; yet grace somehow flowed from that opprobrium in a mysterious way. "But he was wounded for our transgressions, he was bruised for our iniquities; upon him was the chastisement that made us whole, and with his stripes we are healed" (Isa 53:5). That wholeness and healing that transforms our own soul is the essence of redemption.

And so was His pain and complete sacrifice. Christ could have saved us, perhaps, with just a small cut of His finger, or by fasting for a little while, or by simply *willing* to save us. But He and His Father determined a far more demanding and generous way of redeeming us: the bloody and painful Crucifixion, and everything that went with it. This is something that we should never forget if we want to do any real good with our lives. We were not saved by military power, impressive technology, a great economy, or a marvelous speech that someone made once. We were not saved by money, fame, or popularity, either. We were saved by one man dying a painful death, being mocked mercilessly, and shedding all of His blood until only water poured from His side. If we forget this, if we allow ourselves to be comfortable and lukewarm about our faith, we cannot be part of Christ's redemption.

Perhaps you have experienced a great burden or sorrow in life. Maybe you've suffered from some kind of addiction or obsession. What a great relief for you if God has healed you of it, either directly or through others. You may still be tempted, you may feel that old weakness welling up inside of you at times, but with the grace of redemption, you know that you have been healed and that you are not alone anymore. You have begun to experience the "fullness" of Christ and His saving grace coming into you.

The message of the Gospel is truly salvific. As Christ Himself told His Apostles when they were arguing among themselves about matters of preference or place, "the Son of man came not to be served but to serve, and to give his life as a ransom for many" (Matt 20:28). It is that ransom, that free offering of Himself first to God His Father and then to His Apostles and to all men, that is the essence of redemption. He has bought us back from the power of sin and corruption. St. Paul puts this very graphically in his letter to the Ephesians. "And you he made alive, when you were dead through the trespasses and sins in which you once walked, following the course of this world" (2:1–2).

Redemption takes us from a condition of emptiness and despair into a state of grace and hope. It does not depend on our feelings or emotions, but on the action of God's grace in the soul. It begins to heal the hurt and pain that often brings tension between people who should love each other. In speaking of the enmity between Jews and Gentiles, St. Paul affirms that Christ unites both peoples in His salvation: "For he is our peace, who has made us both one, and has broken down the dividing wall of hostility, . . . So then you are no longer strangers and sojourners, but you are fellow citizens with the saints and members of the household of God" (Eph 2:14, 19).

I hope that during your life you have experienced the joy of a good group of friends. They could be from different races and backgrounds, but perhaps you were all involved in some activity that united you: an entertaining sport, a play or social event, an enjoyable conversation, a service project where each one had to contribute something, a study group or seminar, a camping trip or vacation cruise. You all had the same goal, and you were united in mutual friendship and companionship.

Christ's redemption is like that. It unites men and women of many different races, tongues, and backgrounds, and it gives them the same joy and purpose to life. This is the original meaning of the word "catholic," which means "universal"; that is, for everyone and with all the means of salvation. Christ's liberating power not only applies to individual men and women, but extends to the entire human race, and indeed to the whole universe. The Book of Revelation describes this cosmic renewal in vivid terms in chapter 21, which in turn was prophesied in Isaiah 66:22–23. Read it for yourself, and you'll find a treasure of thought and inspiration.

The New Human Race and the Eucharist

As head of the new human race, Jesus Christ reverses what Adam had done as the head of the old human race (see Rom 5:18–21). Sin had produced death, hostility, war, and estrangement between peoples, but with His grace the New Adam brings peace and life once again, reproducing the conditions to obtain paradise for the human race. Of course, this ultimate experience of paradise will not take place until the end of time, but Christ's Church and His redemptive power are working right now on earth to produce it and to set the conditions for its ultimate fulfillment. The holy life of the saints is the prelude to eternal life, and their works anticipate the new heaven and the new earth, which will not come as a result of human progress but of God's providential plan.

No good is ever lost. If what we do on earth is done in Christ, those actions will be transformed and found again in the next life.[1] This means that our actions each day are redemptive insofar as they are connected with Christ the King, who will ultimately deliver the kingdom to His Father (see 1 Cor 15:24).

I remember once speaking with a man who was having a very difficult time with his nineteen-year-old daughter. She was dating a man much older than she, and who was taking advantage of her in many ways. Her father warned her about him, but she insisted that she was in love and would continue seeing him. So the man, a daily attendant at Mass, began "putting his daughter on the paten" (to use his own words), and praying that Christ would illuminate her. At the end of six months, his daughter came up to him and said that she had seen that he was right, and terminated the relationship.

---

[1]   See Second Vatican Council, Pastoral Constitution on the Church in the Modern World *Gaudium et Spes* (December 7, 1965), §39.

Jesus' entire life is summarized in the Eucharist, the ful-fillment of the old Hebrew Passover Feast. We will devote a whole section to the Eucharist later, but it is so essential to salvation that it is worth speaking of it now, at least a little. It was at the Last Supper and on Calvary that our redemp-tion was manifested in the Eucharist and given the power to propagate itself throughout time. In the words of Pope St. John Paul II, "The Eucharist is a straining towards the goal, a foretaste of the fullness of joy promised by Christ (cf. Jn 15:11); it is in some way the anticipation of heaven, the 'pledge of future glory.'"[2]

When we participate in the Mass with devotion, we are identifying ourselves more and more with Christ; we are offering ourselves with God the Son to God the Father in the love of God the Holy Spirit. In a word, the Blessed Trinity is bestowing on us the power to become *co-redeemers*.

This is a far different view of the Mass than as a mere obligation or as a monotonous ceremony. When seen with faith, the Holy Mass is what gives life and hope to the world. For this reason, if we ourselves wish to be "other Christs" and participate in His redemption in the fullest way, we should strive to make the Eucharist the center of our own spiritual life and connect all of our actions with it—which is really the most exciting, fulfilling thing we can do with our lives, though not without pain.

---

[2] Pope St. John Paul II, Encyclical Letter on the Eucharist in Its Relation-ship to the Church *Ecclesia de Eucharistia* (April 17, 2003), §18.

CHAPTER 2

The Church and the
Communion of Saints

"... and behold, I am with you always, to the close of the age." (Matt 28:20)

Jesus did not simply come to the world, redeem us, and then leave us to ourselves. He wanted to be with us always in His Church, which is truly His Mystical Body on earth. Throughout the centuries, He with the Holy Spirit continues to preserve the Church in the truth. He continues to sanctify the human race through the sacraments, which are His sacred and redemptive actions. Each sacrament of the Catholic Church is a sign of what Christ Himself is: a marvelous union of something physical and something divine. Through the Church and her sacraments, Christ continues to redeem the human race and to extend His saving work to people of all different languages and nationalities until the end of time.

This is the deepest identity of the Church. So often we can confuse her with a building, or with certain persons (like the nuns, priests, and bishops), or with certain activities and beliefs. We could confuse the Church with her history, long and complex as it is. Many also confuse her—perhaps ignorantly, perhaps maliciously—with the scandals involving some of her members. But the Church in herself is the people of God, the assembly of all who are saved and are called to enjoy God's presence and love forever. On earth, she is God's principal instrument of redemption since through her men can know what God teaches and how to live holy lives.

St. Cyprian, an ancient writer of the Church, once said: "He can no longer have God for his Father, who has not the Church for his mother."[1] In the Bible, many images are used to describe the Church, and each one has its special meaning. It is called a sheepfold, since Christ the Good Shepherd gathers His own into it; it is called a cultivated field or vineyard, since God Himself cares for and protects it; it is called a building or temple, since it is built upon Christ the Rock and foreshadows the heavenly Jerusalem, the City of God. In a deeper and more mysterious way, Sacred Scripture also calls the Church the Bride of Christ and His Mystical Body; it is Christ who protects and supports her throughout the ages. These images show the closest connection between the Savior and His people. "For just as the body is one and has many members, and all the members of the body, though many, are one body, so it is with Christ" (1 Cor 12:12).

It is precisely because of that closest union with her Founder that the Church is God's instrument of salvation in the world. Though made up of men and women who are sinners, Christ continues to work through her and continues to save the world. Therefore, through faith and the power of the Church's sacraments, Catholic men and women can

---

[1] Cyprian of Carthage, *Treatise 1: On the Unity of the Church*, §6, in *Ante-Nicene* Fathers, vol. 5, trans. Robert Earnest Wallis, ed. Alexander Roberts, James Donaldson, and A. Cleveland Coxe (Buffalo, NY: Christian Literature Publishing Co., 1886.), https://www.newadvent.org/fathers/050701.htm.

truly become co-redeemers. Let's take a quick look at the sacraments to see how they really empower us to be Christ's presence in daily life.

Each one of the sacraments is truly the Savior acting throughout time; they are sensible (that is, sense-able) signs instituted by Him to give grace. Baptism brings a person forgiveness from the guilt of original sin and infuses a new way of existing into him or her that is called sanctifying grace, which is a real participation in God's own life. With this marvelous grace we are transformed from within; we become truly beautiful in God's eyes, and in some way we start to know and love people and things as He Himself does. This is the beginning of salvation for every human being, for without Baptism no person can be justified— whether that be Baptism by water and the word, Baptism of desire, or Baptism of blood. As mentioned in the Introduction, baptized people become another Christ and receive the power to order and direct things on earth to God, to teach the truth about God and salvation to others, and to become a saint through their works, joys, and sufferings. All of these powers configure the baptized person with the Savior Himself and allow him or her to share personally in the mystery of Jesus' redemption.

Confirmation is the strengthening of a soul by the Holy Spirit, who gives a man or woman the fortitude to be a disciple and co-redeemer with Christ in the world and to receive a greater share in His gifts, which were initiated in Baptism. Confirmation is especially important since it fortifies us against temptations of all sorts: giving up the faith, falling into immoral habits, becoming victims of peer pressure. It makes us soldiers of Christ, soldiers who will be able to fight bravely for the Church and for her true teachings instead of going with the flow of relativism and indifference. Though he wasn't speaking of the Sacrament of Confirmation, G. K. Chesterton, the great Catholic apologist at the beginning of the last century, once said: "A dead thing can go with the stream, but only a living thing can go against it."[2] It is Confirmation that makes us truly alive to the Spirit's action, and gives us supernatural courage in the middle of a paganized society.

The Eucharist, as we saw before, is the sacrament par excellence that gives us the very Author of grace; it makes present on the altar the saving sacrifice of Christ and brings Him to us under the appearance of bread and wine. Since it is so important for the mystery of co-redemption, we will devote an entire section to it later on.

Holy Orders gives us the ministers that are needed to propagate Christ's salvation on earth: the deacons, priests, and bishops, with their power of teaching, governing, and sanctifying.

Matrimony gives grace for the sanctification of a man and a woman in a lifetime union. The goal of any holy marriage is for spouses to reach eternal life together as well as to procreate and raise children for the kingdom of God. Holy marriages are essential for the redemption of society; a man and woman who love one another and raise their children to love God are among the greatest co-redeemers on earth.

Anointing of the Sick prepares a person for the final redemptive journey of his or her life so that they can sanctify

---

[2] G. K. Chesterton, *The Everlasting Man* (New York: Dodd, Mead, & Company, 1926), 321.

their illness and come to enjoy the beatific vision. It is the final loving caress that the Church gives to her children in order to ensure their redemption. We will see more later on both Matrimony and the Anointing of the Sick.

The Sacrament of Forgiveness

The Sacrament of Penance, of course, is closely connected with redemption since through it our sins are forgiven and we receive a special grace to conquer our faults. As a co-redeemer, you yourself should love this sacrament and receive it frequently.

The *Catechism of the Catholic Church* recommends frequent Confession because of the great good it does for our souls (see *CCC* 1458). Certainly, if we should commit a mortal sin (a grave offense against God with full knowledge and consent), we should go to Confession as soon as possible to return to God's grace and be able to receive Holy Communion fruitfully. But frequent Confession is most helpful for venial sins also since we receive not only forgiveness but a specific grace to improve.

Sometimes you hear people say that they don't need to go to Confession because they tell their sins directly to God, and they feel they're forgiven. There are two problems with this and, as Christ's apostle to others, you should know how to address them and help people to see the truth.

First of all, how can they be sure that they are forgiven? If a person confesses his sins to an ordained Catholic priest, he knows for sure that he is forgiven because Christ Himself gave this great power to His Apostles when He said: "Receive the Holy Spirit. If you forgive the sins of any, they are forgiven" (John 20:22–23). It would be presumptuous of us to think that God will forgive us automatically when we express sorrow for our sins. But when Almighty God sees His Son in us through the sacrament He instituted, we know that He will surely forgive, in much the same way as a great king will grant pardon to someone if he is asked by his son, whom he loves deeply, to do so.

The second problem is that Catholics who have unforgiven grave sin on their souls should not receive Holy Communion until they bring that sin to the Sacrament of Confession. It would be a sacrilege to receive Christ's Body and Blood with a grave sin on one's soul. Only if there is a serious motive or circumstance involved and it is impossible to go to Confession beforehand can a person receive the Eucharist in this state; but he or she should try to make an act of perfect contrition beforehand. (A perfect act of contrition is to be sorry for our sins, not so much because of the punishment of hell or purgatory, but because they have offended God who is so good). But even in this case, he or she should go to Confession as soon as possible afterward, for this is always the surest way to be forgiven.

To make a good Confession, we need to examine our conscience well. What did we do wrong since our last Confession? Were we proud or vain? Did we curse or use God's name in vain? Did we drink too much, or commit any impurities with ourselves or with another? Did we gossip or speak badly of another? Did we lie or deliberately deceive someone who had the right to know the truth? Were we honest in our work or responsibilities? These are just a few of the questions we can ask ourselves in order to make a good Confession. If you can't think of anything, you can always ask your parish priest or chaplain to ask you questions or to give you a good written examination of conscience, which will help you to identify your sins and confess them clearly.

We also need to be sincerely sorry for our sins in order to make a good Confession. This is an intrinsic part of redemption, for Christ Himself said at the beginning of His ministry, "Repent, and believe the gospel" (Mark 1:15). If we are to be redeemed and help others to be redeemed, we must first of all acknowledge and be sorry for our sins. If we don't do this, Christ's grace and forgiveness cannot enter our souls. Contrition brings with it the sincere desire not to sin again, even if we have a habit of sin that we know will be hard to break. The greater our sorrow and purpose of amendment, the more determined we will be to use all the means we can to avoid sin in the future. To be forgiven in Confession, it is enough that we fear the punishment and consequences of sin—in this life and the next. But with perfect contrition, we are sorry for our sins not only because they deserve purgatory or even hell, as we said before, but above all because they have offended God who is all good.

The third action for a good Confession is just that: to *confess* our sins verbally to the priest, who has the power to forgive sins through Christ Himself. It is humiliating to have to tell our sins to a mere man, who is a sinner like us, yet such is the sacrament that Jesus instituted. Such an action gives us real grace. To make a good Confession we must confess any mortal sins that we've committed since our last Confession, and we should confess them clearly and concisely. That is, we shouldn't make excuses for ourselves but rather say clearly what we have done. If they were grave sins, we should say the approximate number of times we did them.

Lastly, we should do the penance assigned to us by the priest as soon as possible. With the penance (which is often very light and easy to do) we show God that we are truly sorry for our sins, and that we want to make atonement for them.

When we go to Confession frequently and confess our sins sincerely and humbly, we experience a great peace of soul. Redemption has truly reached us, as it did to so many persons that Jesus touched in the Gospels, such as Peter, Mary Magdalene, and Zacchaeus. Jesus the Good Shepherd awaits us in this holy sacrament. He wants to take us into His arms and bind our wounds, then carry us safely on His shoulders.

Let's give Him the opportunity often to do this with us. And let's encourage our friends to do the same, especially those who have been away from the sacraments for a long time. It is a great work of mercy, and a truly co-redemptive act, to help someone be reconciled to God by confessing his or her sins humbly. While only they can actually repent in their heart and go to Confession, we can certainly assist them by our prayers and encouraging words, perhaps even by giving them a good examination of conscience to read.

Finally, Confession not only brings grace and forgiveness to us as individuals but "reconciles us with the Church" herself (see *CCC* 1469). Every sin, whether mortal or venial, is like a wound in the Body of Christ. It both hurts our soul and damages our communion with the Church. Confession restores us to communion with the Church and prepares us in a certain way for the final judgment at the end of time. In other words, forgiveness and reconciliation have effects beyond our own souls: they re-establish harmony between us and all people, and even creation itself. Pope St. John Paul II explains this profound process in his apostolic exhortation on Penance: "The forgiven penitent is reconciled with himself in his inmost being, where he regains his own true identity. He is reconciled with his brethren whom he has in some way attacked and wounded. He is reconciled with the church. He is reconciled with all creation."[3]

Living Members of Christ's Body

Jesus did not establish a dull or passive Church but an active, transforming one. Therefore, each one of us must do our part since the Church is not simply the hierarchy or the religious. We are all called to be *co-redeemers*: each one of us, through our prayers, friendships, works, and sufferings, must be other Christs who bring His kingdom to the world. For this reason, we need to know the Church's teachings well—not only on current issues such as human life, social justice, and the family, but on profound topics such as prayer, the Incarnation, and grace. In this way we become deeper friends of Christ and we communicate His light and truth to others.

It is true that other religions, especially Christian ones, have many elements of truth and goodness within them. Many Protestant preachers give more motivating homilies and sermons than Catholic priests. Many Protestant believers know the Bible, chapter and verse, better than many Catholics. Many non-Catholic Christians sing better than

[3]   Pope St. John Paul II, Post-Synodal Apostolic Exhortation on Reconciliation and Penance in the Mission of the Church Today *Reconciliatio et Paenitentia* (December 2, 1984), §31, no. 5.

we do. And some are more pro-family and pro-life than many Catholics, though this would not be the case if all Catholics were true to their faith.

And yet there is only one Savior of mankind, and He founded only one Church. A good friend and convert from Protestantism told me, shortly after he and his family were received into the Catholic Church, that they were overjoyed because they had received the Sacraments of Penance, Confirmation, and Communion; at last, they had experienced the "fullness" of the Church. The one true Church indeed has the fullness of the sacraments—all seven of them—corresponding to the different phases of our life. She has the fullness of revelation, with its twofold source in Scripture and Tradition; she has the fullness of certainty about that revelation since the pope and the bishops in union with him have preserved intact all the truths that Christ has revealed with the help of the Holy Spirit; she has the fullness of grace, not only through the sacraments but also through the intercession of the Mother of Christ and the saints for each one of us.

At times, you hear people claim that they don't need an "organized" Church to be saved. They say that they simply try to lead a good life themselves, and if they sin, they tell their sins directly to God. This can sound very authentic and personal at first, but it is really quite presumptuous (as we said before), and not a little foolish. It presumes, first of all, that these people can save themselves through their good actions, and that somehow God has to take notice of these. Why? What makes them so important that God has to listen to them, or reward them for their actions, which may or may not be good? Or why should He forgive them simply because they tell their sins to Him? Rather, wouldn't God be more offended because these people have deliberately spurned the visible and organized Church that He founded, established in the sacrifice and blood of His Son? Rejecting an organized and visible Church is a lot like rejecting a ladder given to you to help climb out of a pit into which you have fallen. The ladder is there and very practical for you to use. There are sacraments, places of worship, a visible structure of authority, clear teachings, and laws for the good of believers. How foolish to try to climb out of the pit—to rise to heaven—in some other way; it can only lead to disaster.

The Catholic Church answers the deepest desires of the human heart. It provides a profound peace and hope, along with the highest moral standards for human conduct. It is filled with mystery, yet it is also very practical and down to earth. The Church's sacraments combine matter and spirit since we are a union of both these things. It gives the deepest meaning and purpose to human suffering, and at the same time provides the greatest consolation for those who suffer in union with Christ. It acknowledges clearly the evil in the world and in ourselves but does not cease to offer forgiveness and hope in the middle of it. It enkindles the greatest experiences of joy in the human heart, along with a spirit of adventure and even romance. Above all, the Church gives its members the love of God, which has become incarnate in Jesus Christ.

Look at the lives of the great saints and their complete service to the Church: St. Agnes, who pledged her virginity to Christ at an early age and preferred to die rather than to betray it; St. Patrick, who returned to evangelize the very people who had enslaved him as a boy; St. Francis Xavier, who set the whole Far Eastern world ablaze with his courageous preaching of the Gospel; St. Mother Teresa of Calcutta, who served Christ Himself in the poorest of the poor.

From these examples we see clearly that the effort to be truly faithful to the Church can take many forms. At times it is simply prayer for others—for the innocent, for the unborn, for world peace. At other times it will be sacrifice and penance, as when we offer an extra bit of work or when we fast in order to win graces for a friend who's in trouble. At still other times it could be conversing about God and the sacraments with someone who does not know of them, or defending the Church if she or her members are being unjustly attacked. All of these are legitimate ways of being the hands, feet, and arms of Christ—His tongue as well. They spring from the power of our Baptism, when we were configured to Christ Himself, and received the mission of witnessing His truth, ordering the things of this world to God, and bringing grace to those around us.

And it is the Holy Spirit who enlivens these gifts within us through the Sacrament of Confirmation, inspiring us to act as kings and prophets like Christ and to have a truly priestly soul.

The Network of Grace

When speaking of redemption, we could perhaps think that we can save ourselves or others by our own virtue or willpower. Or we could concentrate exclusively on our own salvation. Both paths would be mistaken since redemption and co-redemption derive their power from complete identification with Christ, who was truly the *man for others*. Pope Benedict in his second encyclical *Saved in Hope* (*Spe Salvi*) put it this way: "The relationship with Jesus, however, is a relationship with the one who gave himself as a ransom for all (cf. *1 Tim* 2:6). Being in communion with Jesus Christ draws us into his 'being for all'; it makes it our own way of being. He commits us to live for others, but only through communion with him does it become possible truly to be there for others, for the whole."[4]

A believer in Jesus Christ and His Church is never alone. Whether we are the pilgrim Church on earth, the Church being purified in purgatory, or the Church triumphant in heaven—we are all connected by a common source of grace and power. We are all united in the Body of Christ. This is called the communion of saints. Christ did not form a Church made up of independent individuals who do everything by themselves and who never need anyone's help. Even if at times it may seem that we are the only ones defending the Church or a moral truth where we live or work, we are actually supported and sustained by others continually.

No co-redeemer is ever alone. First, if we are in the state of grace, the Holy Trinity Itself is dwelling within us—Father, Son, and Holy Spirit. We also have the prayer of the Blessed Mother for us, along with our guardian angel, who has the special mission of protecting us from harm and getting us to heaven. And if this were not enough, we have the saints who intercede for us, especially our patron saint or angel, after whom we are named, or one of the saints to whom we have a special devotion.

The Church exists in both time and eternity, and her co-redemptive action permeates them both. As we pray to

---

[4] Pope Benedict XVI, Encyclical Letter on Christian Hope *Spe Salvi* (November 30, 2007), §28.

the saints in heaven, we also pray for the Church suffering in purgatory. One of the greatest acts of co-redemption that we can perform is to liberate a person who is suffering in purgatory and cannot therefore be with God because of some attachment to sin or punishment due to sin.

The Church, like a loving mother, has a multitude of graces and personal help for such people in need. One such help are indulgences. Indulgences are drawn from the rich treasury of prayers and good works entrusted by God to her care and distribution; namely, the infinite value of Christ's death on the Cross united with the merits of His mother and those of all the saints throughout the centuries (see *CCC* 1476–77). By performing a specific act of penance or devotion and fulfilling certain other conditions like prayer for the intentions of the Holy Father and the reception of Confession and Holy Communion, a person can gain the remission of temporal punishments due to sin, either for himself or for those who are deceased.

To gain an indulgence for a deceased person is a most powerful means of co-redemption because it removes the final obstacles between a person and God either partially or completely. A person can gain a plenary indulgence for a soul in purgatory between November 1 and 8 if he visits a cemetery, prays for a deceased person, and fulfills the other conditions needed for a plenary indulgence, including detachment from all venial sin. Some of the more common indulgences include visits to certain shrines and holy places, the offering of one's work each day, the family Rosary, and the praying of the Way of the Cross.[5]

---

[5] For a complete list of indulgences and their requirements you can

In addition to the indulgences we can gain for ourselves and the deceased, we have the prayer and support of many Catholics who are still on earth and who are also trying to be true to the Church and her teachings in their own circumstances, perhaps very similar to ours. As we read in the letter of James, "The prayer of a righteous man has great power in its effects" (Jas 5:16). Though Christ is the sole source of grace and justification, He wanted that grace and justification to reach us through the prayers and good works of others; thus, the communion of saints—an immense and fascinating network of love working in and beyond time.

This "cloud of witnesses" (Heb 12:1) is also one of the most exciting truths about the Catholic Church, and it stands at the heart of the mystery of co-redemption.

The Church as founded by Christ is indefectible, that is, she will never disappear but will continue to exist in a glorious way forever. Scripture affirms this fact in the vision of the New Jerusalem in the Book of Revelation. "'Behold, the dwelling of God is with men. He will dwell with them, and they shall be his people, and God himself will be with them; he will wipe away every tear from their eyes, and death shall be no more.' . . . And he who sat upon the throne said, 'Behold, I make all things new'" (Rev 21:3–5). The fulfillment of the Church is what God had planned from all eternity: the fullness of the Church is the gathering of a great multitude of human beings into God's own life with a joy that will never end.

In summary, the Church in herself is a tremendous

consult the *Enchiridion of Indulgences* or the more condensed *Handbook of Indulgences*, both put out by Catholic Book Publishing.

mystery. She is destined for final fulfillment only in heaven, at the end of time. She is a pilgrim on earth, yet has within herself an everlasting principle of life through her sacraments. She is both visible, in her temples and members, yet she is invisible in the grace that she brings to all men. She has a divine truth given to her, yet she must always be fighting to maintain that truth both for those within her and outside of her.

Defending the Church

An important part of co-redemption is to promote and *defend* Christ's Body on earth, which is His Church: one, holy, catholic, and apostolic.

The Church is the sacrament of God's presence on earth. "He who hears you hears me" (Luke 10:16). Jesus said this to His Apostles, and He meant it. The Church proclaims the truth about the things that really matter: human life and dignity, the real meaning of freedom, sexuality and marriage, care for the poor, and, above all, how to obtain eternal life. This is her mission, given to her by her Founder, and it will continue to be her mission until the end of time.

And yet, because of sin and selfishness, many people do not want to hear these truths. They would prefer that the Church be silent. Some even want to destroy her. These enemies of the Church (though she really has no enemies—they make themselves her enemies) have pervasive power in our country today. They have great influence in academia—yes, including many college professors—and they consistently present the history of the Church in a negative way or deliberately neglect to speak of her immense accomplishments for the last two thousand years. The Church has fostered science, established hospitals to care for the sick, educated the most neglected members of society, and constantly defended the freedom and dignity of each human person against materialistic and atheistic forces.

The secular media often presents a one-sided and quite prejudiced view of the Catholic Church. Besides completely forgetting her spiritual and moral purpose, many newspapers and internet sources continually harp upon the scandals in the Church, especially involving priests and bishops, even for offenses committed many years ago. Few media sources speak of the good and positive contributions that many priests, bishops, religious, and Catholic lay people have done and are doing for the country—including the moral education of young people, care for the poor and the sick, and especially the compassionate defense of the lives of unborn children, who are being destroyed by the millions each year.

In the 1940s and 50s, one could occasionally see a movie that presented Christianity and the Church in a positive and inspiring way. But after 1965, we would be hard-pressed to find such films. Nowadays, Hollywood blatantly refuses to produce a pro-Christian movie, and if occasionally they do produce a film that has Catholics or Christians in it, they are often portrayed as corrupt, unnatural, or weird. In many modern films, Christian morals, especially sexual morals, are made to look old-fashioned or prudish. Hardly ever will you find praise or even interest for what really keeps our society together: honest, hardworking persons and authentic families composed of a father, mother, and children.

There is nothing new about the persecution of Christianity. It has been going on for two thousand years—in different ways, some violent, some more subtle. If we accept the prophecies in the Book of Revelation, this battle between good and evil will continue until the end of time, when at last the Antichrist will come, whom the Lamb of God will slay and cast with all of his followers into hell. In the meantime, we must be prepared to be misunderstood and attacked throughout the centuries. This, too, is part of the mystery of redemption, and the mystery of the Church as Christ's suffering Body on earth.

We are called to be co-redeemers in that Church. Therefore, we cannot be complacent: we need to have an excellent formation in our faith and be aware of all the errors and attacks against it. We cannot let ourselves be deceived by popular slogans and buzzwords. Even more, we should have prompt and clear answers for attacks or misunderstandings, whether they be from an atheistic or agnostic teacher or from a friend who is sincerely confused.

In football, they say that the best defense is a good offense. The Catholic *Catechism* with its abundant Scripture references, as well as the writings of Popes John Paul II, Benedict XVI, and Francis, are excellent primary sources. Let's also be sure to have up-to-date and well-reasoned Catholic books at hand, especially of apologetics, and be aware of useful websites like Catholic Answers' Catholic. com that provide valuable strategies and information for presenting the truth of the faith.

With a positive attitude, we will also try to bring clear and saving ideas to strong influencers of public opinion, as we mentioned before. Christ said, "Let your light . . . shine," and "You are the salt of the earth" (see Matt 5:13–16). We cannot abandon the field of public opinion or politics to people with non-Christian ideologies. By working in the media, academics, or government, we can each of us spread the truth of Christ in a creative and expansive way. This includes, of course, a helpful use of technology.

Co-redemption can be multiplied electronically through Facebook, Twitter, and social media in general. (Although we need to be aware of the internal biases these media can have.) People nowadays pour out their souls and ideas to people thousands of miles away . . . whether for better or for worse. But with grace we can turn electronic messages into gold, for they can be great opportunities for real witnessing to Christ and His truth: there are some moving stories of conversions through electronics. I know of one college student who was able to attract his girlfriend to the Catholic faith by a good use of his smartphone. They would often have discussions, phones in hand, but he had the better quotes and websites; with the help of the Holy Spirit, she became convinced that the evidence was in her boyfriend's favor, and she is now a Catholic.

The works of C. S. Lewis, G. K. Chesterton, and Hilaire Belloc are attractively written and have true Christian content that has instructed and moved many people for nearly one hundred years. So are the works of St. John Henry Newman, recently canonized by the Church. Many people have book discussion clubs and seminars in their parishes or homes to go more deeply into the ideas of these and other writers. Others attend conferences and talks at the Catholic ministry centers on the campuses of certain colleges and universities. All these activities build solidarity with fellow believers as well as confidence in evangelizing.

A final caution. In speaking with others, we must never

forget St. Paul's famous expression: "*veritatem facientes in caritate*"; that is, we must speak the truth with love (Eph 4:15). A strictly confrontational approach will not work; as a matter of fact, it often produces hostility because people's pride can be hurt, and they feel they must defend their opinion. We must understand that many people, including our friends or colleagues, have not had an experience of God or a spiritual conversion in their lives, or they have never been exposed to a clear presentation of moral truth or the Church's teachings. Many have heard only deformed or negative things about morality and the Church. For this reason, we must first of all pray for those in error and give them the charity of Christ by our kindness and sincere interest in them.

Oftentimes this charity is more powerful than any intellectual argument you could give. It's important to listen sincerely to their ideas and to try to understand and appreciate the truth in them. Some of their reflections born of life experiences may be much deeper than our own. What we cannot do is to have the mentality of "circling the wagons" and simply protecting ourselves or our own families. We must have the faith and courage to meet many people and listen to them, even if they are "on the peripheries," as Pope Francis often says. This is certainly what Our Lord, the Good Shepherd, meant when He told His disciples to "go . . . and make disciples of all nations, . . . teaching them to observe all that I have commanded you" (Matt 28:19–20). Christ's message of salvation is for all individuals and peoples.

All that being said, after hearing and trying to understand the people we are seeking to evangelize, we cannot compromise when it comes to moral truth and the permanence of the Church and her teachings. To quote from an ancient Christian letter, "The Church is in the world like the soul in the body."[6] In other words, it is the Church that gives life and direction to the world, and not the opposite. She is the conscience of the world, and despite all the errors and sins of her members—both priests and lay people—she remains the spotless bride of Christ. *Without the Church, the world would collapse.*

[6] "The Epistle of Mathetes to Diognetus," ca. second century AD.

CHAPTER 3

Faith

"Jesus said to him, 'You have believed because you have seen me. Blessed are those who have not seen and yet believe.'" (John 20:29)

WE SHOULD BE VERY GRATEFUL to St. Thomas for his stubbornness. He wanted to touch the side of Christ with his hand and put his finger into His wounds in order to be convinced that it was truly His body, the same one that had suffered on the Cross. His conclusion, when he says, "My Lord and my God!" (John 20:28), expresses what we should always believe as members of His Church on earth. Unlike Thomas, we did not touch the risen body of Christ personally; yet, we believe through the testimony of the Apostles and the constant witnessing of the Church.

Faith is absolutely essential for redemption and the spiritual life. The Savior makes it a condition for His doing miracles, and St. Paul says that "without faith it is impossible to please [God]" (Heb 11:6). This has a very practical meaning for us who would like to become co-redeemers: we may know many things, reach the top of our class or profession, gain the admiration of thousands of people, but if we lack faith, we cannot know God or receive His saving love into our hearts. At times we may have to say, "Increase our faith!" (Luke 17:5), as the disciples did with Jesus.

But what is faith? The *Catechism of the Catholic Church*, quoting St. Thomas Aquinas in his *Summa Theologiae*, describes it as an "act of the intellect assenting to the divine truth by command of the will moved by God through grace" (*CCC* 155). That's a rather dense and involved statement, but if we analyze it properly, we can understand it.

First, we note that faith is not a natural or human virtue we can acquire through our own effort, such as good time management or skill in speaking. Faith is a gift of God by which we are able to believe in Jesus and His Church and the power of His redemption. It is not the assent of our mind to something that we have figured out by ourselves, like a history question or mathematical equation.

Second, our will or desire has a lot to do with it. Since the grace of faith is mysterious and beyond our reason, it somehow *moves our wills to desire it* and to command our minds to assent to God's revelation. In this way it is quite different from science, human opinion, and even human faith by which we believe others and what they tell us about themselves or the world—though it is true that parents, friends, and good teachers can lead us to the true faith through their guidance and example.

Faith is given to us at Baptism, either as small children or adults, when God's own life and grace are infused into our souls and we become part of His family. This is really the moment that we are *born again*. The rest of our life should conform to that baptismal grace. As mentioned in the introduction to this book, we receive in our souls the salvific mission of Christ Himself, which enables us to *teach*, to *sanctify*, and to *govern* the world with Him. These three gifts solidify our personal calling to be co-redeemers with Christ, who bring His kingdom to those around us.

Faith therefore is not the result of our own reflection, nor is it some kind of emotion or elated feeling. Many people make this mistake. They think that they are being truly religious if they are "charged up" about a certain idea or project. Or they will judge the Church on the basis of their feelings or enthusiasm (or lack thereof) when listening to a homily or receiving a sacrament. The gift of faith goes deeper than this. Though at times it may include feelings and enthusiasm, faith does not need these things, since its source is God's grace that moves us to believe in His Word.

Similarly, faith is not a production of the subconscious mind that needs to assign a meaning to life and therefore invents a God, as some modern rationalists have claimed. On the contrary, faith is actually a gift infused into our souls by God; it comes from *outside* of us. It is a supernatural capacity to believe in God's revelation and His Church, which of course needs to grow in us throughout our life, always with the help of divine grace.

At times, Catholics can get confused between their faith in Christ and that of Protestants. Often Protestants will appear to have more faith than we do because they are more energetic and confident in their being saved. They claim that it is enough for them to "believe in Jesus Christ as their personal Savior," and they are convinced of their salvation. Yet this type of faith can easily become presumptuous if there is no attempt to live a good Christian life or resist temptation. It is a conviction that seems to depend more on a person's desire to believe, but it does not really transform him or her from within. Catholics believe in a true transformation and sanctification of the soul through grace. Faith is a free gift from God, and we are saved by that gift along with God's saving love, which really penetrates and elevates our soul. Of course, we must correspond and try to grow in faith each day, but ultimately it is God's grace that saves us, not our own personal conviction or trust that we are saved. This is a key difference between the Protestant view of faith and salvation and the teachings of the Catholic Church.

Sin also eats away at our faith. If we insist on reading books opposed to the Catholic faith without any attempt to refute them or see their errors, we can easily lose our belief in the Church and in Christ. If we develop immoral habits, such as drinking to excess or sexual sins, we can end up denying that there is a moral law or even a God behind that law. Peer pressure can also undermine our belief in God or produce a false sense of acceptance—for homosexual actions or abortion for instance. Nobody, especially among young people, wants to be rejected socially, or be considered "uncool." Certainly nobody wants to be called judgmental or unjust, which can happen when we defend basic moral standards about sexuality. This is particularly the case of the LBGT agenda that is so pervasive right now in our country; if anyone dares to say that homosexual acts are morally wrong, or that same-sex marriage is not real marriage, he or she will be branded as intolerant and discriminated against, even to the point of losing their job. The same is true for people who disagree with so-called "gender affirming" operations for transgender individuals.

But the fact of not following or defending moral standards has far worse consequences: we end up doing nothing to help society, and our perception of right and wrong—and that of many others around us—can be radically corrupted.

There will be times in everyone's life when our faith appears to weaken: this could be due to the bad example of people around us, doubts in our own mind, the existence of evil and tragedy in the world (this particularly can hurt the faith of people), even questionings or insinuations planted inside of us by the devil, who doesn't want us to believe. On those occasions, we must say more courageously, "I believe; help my unbelief!" (Mark 9:24). Though we don't understand why He has permitted something, though we may be hurt and scandalized by the sins and errors of fellow Christians and Catholics, though our minds cannot explain the fact of evil in the world, the great gift of faith assists us. Faith is a firm belief not only in Christ as our Savior, but also in His Church, which is indefectible. Then He can work the miracle of His grace and conversion within us and others.

It is not that faith goes against reason or science. This has been an attack for centuries by nonbelievers of all different stripes, from skeptics to rationalists. But it's an attack based on a false dichotomy that opposes the knowledge given by science and the knowledge given by faith. Faith transcends the conclusions of reason and science but does not contradict them. As Christ's apostles, we must be ready to demonstrate this and to show the true meaning of faith to those around us.

Some of the greatest scientists in history, including non-Catholics, after making significant discoveries in their research, have admitted that they are just beginning to learn about how the universe works, and the rest is mystery. God indeed is a mystery, but He does not contradict Himself, for

He is the One who created the universe and man's reason, and also the One who revealed the content of faith. Both faith and reason really help and complement one another, as Pope St. John Paul II stated so elegantly in his encyclical *Faith and Reason* (*Fides et Ratio*).

A very moving example of faith is that of Bartimaeus, the blind beggar of Jericho (see Mark 10:46–52). This poor man, blind from birth, one day heard a huge crowd passing in front of him, and learned that they were following Jesus of Nazareth. With the spark of faith inside he began to shout at the top of his lungs, "Jesus, Son of David, have mercy on me!" (Mark 10:47). Some people in the crowd tried to silence him, the Gospel tells us. Perhaps they were annoyed by his loud voice, or perhaps some were enemies of Christ and did not want Him to do another miracle. But the more they tried to silence him, the louder Bartimaeus shouted for Christ.

There is a message here for us. Many forces in society around us do not want us to believe. There will be multiple signs, subtle or not so subtle, that people do not want to hear about Christ and His life. They really don't want Jesus to perform a miracle, or His Church to succeed. So they will try to stifle the voice of faith—either by ironic and indirect criticisms, or by open hostility. Often they will claim that faith violates the separation of church and state, which is not truthful, and which comes from a biased reading of the First Amendment of the U.S. Constitution. But if we are to be true co-redeemers, we must keep speaking and living according to the teachings of Christ anyway.

A Faith That Is Informative and Performative

Here we enter an important consideration: the difference between an informative faith and a performative faith. As co-redeemers we should have both. Pope Benedict dealt with this distinction in his second encyclical, *Saved in Hope*. Speaking of the witness of the early Christians, he said, "Christianity was not only 'good news'—the communication of a hitherto unknown content. In our language we would say: the Christian message was not only 'informative' but 'performative.'"[1]

Put very simply, we must not only believe certain things to be true but we must act accordingly. Yes, I believe that there are three Persons in one God (an article in the Catholic Creed), but I should also make the effort to pray to them and get to know each one. Yes, I believe that Christian marriage is indissoluble since it is the reflection of Christ's own love for His Church, but I must also believe in the grace of marriage and how it enables couples to love one another truly, to have children, and raise them in the faith. Yes, I believe that Christ is truly present in the Eucharist (Body, Blood, Soul, and Divinity), but I must also make an effort to speak with Him frequently in the tabernacle and to receive Him into my body and soul as often as I can. This is truly an operative faith, not simply a theoretical one.

The same thing applies to our entire view of history and human events. They are not simply the result of chance or of "might makes right." Rather, we believe that behind the

[1] Pope Benedict XVI, Encyclical Letter on Christian Hope *Spe Salvi* (November 30, 2007), §2.

events of history there is a personal and loving God—despite all the conflicts and tragedies of human existence. With such a faith in God's providence, we can be truly free, as Pope Benedict states in his encyclical: "It is not the elemental spirits of the universe, the laws of matter, which ultimately govern the world and mankind, but a personal God governs the stars, that is, the universe; it is not the laws of matter and of evolution that have the final say, but reason, will, love—a Person. And if we know this Person and he knows us, then truly the inexorable power of material elements no longer has the last word; we are not slaves of the universe and its laws, we are free."[2]

Faith frees us, therefore, from any kind of pessimism or skepticism.

Putting Ourselves in the Gospel Scenes

By considering carefully the scenes from the Gospel, even by putting ourselves into them as an eyewitness, so to speak, we can learn more about our response of faith to the redemptive Christ. Consider Peter's faith, which at certain moments was solid like a rock, but at other times became weakened by fear and human concerns. In other words, in his mind he believed in Christ and His power, but his emotions and reactions were not in sync with what he believed. For instance, in the famous incident of Peter's going to Christ over the water, he was actually walking on the water for a time, but then he allowed his fear of the wind and the waves to overcome him, and Jesus had to save him (see Matt 14:31). So often in our

[2] Pope Benedict XVI, *Spe Salvi*, §5.

lives, the same can happen to us: we know the truths of the Church and the faith, but peer pressure, public opinion, and human respects can cause us to doubt. The minute we take our eyes and mind away from Christ, we begin to sink.

For this reason, there will be many times in our life when we will have to admit a lack of faith, or we will have to go to Christ begging for the grace to believe more. We may do this with deeds. In the powerful words of St. James, "Faith apart from works is dead" (Jas 2:26). When our faith leads to action, we are building our house upon a rock, to use another image from the Gospel, and not upon sand. Those deeds could be, for instance, the giving of our time to God each day in prayer, specific service to those in need, the offering of our daily work, the conscientious study of the Catholic faith—and our courageous defense of it when needed.

At times, there can be a good "shamelessness" in manifesting our faith. Consider the very powerful example of the leper who went up to Jesus one day—actually blocking His way on the road—and said: "Lord, if you will, you can make me clean" (Matt 8:2). A leper was truly an outcast in that ancient society and other societies throughout history. Since the disease is so contagious, lepers would live together in caves and remote areas far from the towns and cities. Good people would leave them food and other provisions on a rock, then run away. Whenever a leper would walk down a road, he would have to shout "Unclean! Unclean!" or else fasten a bell around his neck to alert people of the danger. Remembering these circumstances, we can appreciate the incredible boldness of this particular leper. He had surely heard of Jesus' healing powers, and somehow he had heard that He was close by, very similar to Bartimaeus of Jericho whom we saw before.

His approach is direct because his need is so evident: "Lord, if you will, you can make me clean." And Jesus' answer to him is just as direct and personal: "I will; be clean" (Mt 8:3). The Gospel adds that Jesus actually touched the leper, something unheard of and quite dangerous. But Christ's love conquers all dangers, and the power of the leper's simple and humble faith deeply moves His heart. We should ask ourselves if we have that same humble faith in approaching Christ with our needs. Too often we can be tempted to "figure things out" by ourselves, or hold back in making a commitment to God or the Church. Perhaps we're afraid of losing something by giving Him everything, or pride makes us want to look good or keep something for ourselves. The bold and beautiful faith of the leper is a great lesson for us if we ourselves are troubled by unclean thoughts or bitter feelings. If we cannot overcome these things by our own power, let's have the operative faith of the leper, trusting in Christ's unfailing love for us and His desire to heal us no matter how sick or wretched we are.

A Leap in the Dark?

People often compare faith to a leap in the darkness. There is a certain element of truth to this. If we could figure out God and His plans, we would no longer need to have faith or trust in Him. But by definition, revelation is beyond the human mind since it proceeds from a divine mind. Therefore, we will always need to take a jump into the obscurity, so to speak.

Yet faith is not all darkness; it is also a light that helps to see things. Many conversions take place little by little as people are gradually led to see the greatness of the Church and her teachings or they come to admire persons who truly live a Christian life. This happens in many marriages and close friendships. It also happens with people who read and research a lot; they come to the realization that the Catholic Church is truly divine and has received God's revelation. Often, there is no one perceptible moment of conversion, as in the case of St. Paul. Rather, a person, with the help of God's grace, gradually comes to this awareness: *I need to believe, I want to believe.*

Perhaps we could phrase it this way: the more we believe, the more truths we see. For instance, the mystery of redemption is indeed beyond our comprehension. How grace can enter and convert a person, turning him from being a sinner into a holy man, is beyond human understanding. And yet, the more we believe in God's grace and the real conversions of people, the more we will see both things taking place around us. The more a couple believes in the grace of Matrimony, the closer they will be to one another and will help each other to find God. The more a priest or dedicated layperson believes in the great gift of celibacy, the more he will appreciate and live it and the closer he will come to that complete gift of self to the love that never ends. The more we believe in the Trinity, in the three divine Persons who have created us and who sustain all things, the more we are led to pray to them and distinguish each Person in our minds and hearts.

If we are to be redeemed as persons, we have to allow Christ's love and grace to enter our souls and, yes, to believe in His Word and His power to save us. Then we can truly be co-redeemers who help our family and friends to believe as well. Jesus many times challenged His Apostles to think with faith and real ambition: "If you have faith as a grain of mustard seed, you will say to this mountain, 'Move from here to there,' and it will move; and nothing will be impossible to you" (Matt 17:20) His last words were words of challenge and trust in Him at the same time: "Go therefore and make disciples of all nations . . . and behold, I am with you always, to the close of the age" (Matt 28:19–20). Imagine how much faith those disciples had in order to fulfill that command: with very few means and resources they went to different nations and cultures, and, ultimately, they sacrificed their lives while transmitting His teachings.

In the same way, if we want to be followers of Christ, we must truly believe in Him and commit ourselves to a *new* way of thinking and acting. We have to believe that Christ and His Spirit can really make us happy as well as holy and that we can bring hundreds, even thousands of people into the Church, which is His Body on earth. In the words of the Apostle himself, "I can do all things in him who strengthens me" (Phil 4:13). Faith is the supernatural gift that gives us both the light and energy to spread the truth and love of Christ, and often, to swim against the current in order to do it.

Let's close this section with a quote from Pope Benedict at World Youth Day in Australia, 2008: "To be truly alive is to be transformed from within, open to the energy of God's love. In accepting the power of the Holy Spirit you too can transform your families, communities and nations."[3] That transforming power is not a product of human knowledge or ingenuity; it has a divine source that enables us to see where others do not see, and to risk going where others dare not go.

[3] Pope Benedict XVI, "Address of His Holiness Benedict XVI" (World Youth Day, Vigil with the Young People, Randwick Racecourse, Sydney, Australia, July 19, 2008).

CHAPTER 4

Prayer

"Not as I will, but as you will." (Matt 26:39)

IN HIS PRAYER AT THE GARDEN OF GETHSEMANE, Christ gives us the model of all prayer. It is personal, it is sincere, and it concludes by conforming the human will to God's. For this reason we can say that His prayer is truly redemptive since it brings together man's will (His own at this moment) with the divine will. Let's always remember that the cause of man's sin and alienation was disobedience in the first place. If we are to be co-redeemers, our own prayer also must end in union with God's will.

During His public ministry, Christ told His followers that "they ought always to pray and not lose heart" (Luke 18:1). Most people would admit that they pray at times—for instance, in emergencies, or in a surge of strong feelings or emotions. But if we want our prayer to be redemptive, and to be a constant witness to Christ in our lives, we need to pray daily, both in easy times and hard times. This will literally keep us connected to His mind and heart, and our actions will little by little become His. We will also be much freer and happier since continual prayer unites us to God's goodness and truth, which is the goal of our life. Good actions that truly reconcile the world with God will follow.

By daily prayer you will discover who you should be and

what you should be doing. It is easy to go through life drifting from one experience to another, never really knowing where we're going, like an autumn leaf tossed here and there by the wind. But with daily prayer you will grow in faith and happiness because you will actually be living with Jesus throughout the day—whether at work, with your families, or with your friends. More than that, prayer will show you the way not only to talk to Jesus but to *fall in love with Him*.

Yes, falling in love. In choosing a spouse, don't people need to spend time with one another? Why shouldn't it be the same with loving God? "Love at first sight" happens rarely, and even when it happens, time is needed to correct any blind spots. To fall in love with Christ, we therefore need to pray every day, giving Him our time generously. In this way we will not only contemplate God's truth and goodness more clearly—which is the first result of personal prayer—but we also will be able to spread His kingdom on earth. As the old adage from classical philosophy states, "*nemo dat quod non habet*": no one gives what he does not have.

A good way to begin your day is with a morning offering. It need not be a long prayer, but it should focus your entire day on doing God's will and giving glory to Him. A good formula might be: "O my God, I offer you all my prayers, works, joys, and sufferings of this day, in union with your Most Sacred Heart and the Holy Sacrifice of the Mass." That prayer, or different forms of it, can be repeated throughout the day, for instance, in starting your work at home, at school, or in the office. In this way you'll be living God's presence at every moment, in union with the Incarnate Christ who also had a home and a job and social contacts. You'll be transforming society little by little.

Kinds of Prayer

Liturgical prayer is the most powerful kind of prayer since it is directly connected with the events of our salvation. For this reason Holy Mass, as we shall see, is the most powerful prayer we can offer because it is the redemptive prayer and sacrifice of Christ renewed every day on the altar. Our own prayer, whether it be praise or petition, is magnified and made effective when united with His Body and Blood. The prayers related to the other sacraments are not only instructive but also sanctifying because they insert us into the mystery of grace that is happening at that moment. "What do you seek from the Church?" the priest asks parents and godparents at the beginning of the baptismal liturgy. And their answer: "faith." And so it is with the words and actions surrounding all the sacraments: the exchange of the marriage vows, the words of the bishop as he ordains new priests, the tender words of support and love surrounding the Anointing of the Sick.

At certain times of the year, such as on great feast days and liturgical seasons like Christmas and Easter, the faithful can enhance and enrich their prayer. The days immediately before or after the great solemnities of the Church are also marvelous times of greater prayer in union with all the faithful: for instance, the novena before the Feast of the Immaculate Conception (December 8), the ten-day devotion to the Holy Spirit before Pentecost, the Octave following the Solemnity of Corpus Christi, and many others.

But the greatest liturgical prayer will always be the ceremonies of Holy Week, the week of our redemption. From Palm Sunday to Easter Sunday, the Church's liturgy presents the major events of our salvation: the betrayal of Christ, the establishment of the Eucharist and the priesthood, the anguished prayer of Jesus in Gethsemane, the bloody Crucifixion, the descent into hell, the glorious victory of Easter Sunday—which is preceded by the lighting of the Easter candle during the Easter vigil service, the baptism of the catechumens (an ancient Christian tradition), and the singing of the Alleluia once again.

Holy Week is really the remembrance and reenactment of the major events of our redemption. It summarizes the culmination of Christ's life on earth, and through its liturgy it helps us to remember—and in some way participate in—the great Paschal Mystery of Christ; that is, Our Lord's ultimate victory over man's two greatest enemies: sin and death.

Prayer can be either vocal or silent, in community or by ourselves. A full life of prayer will have all four elements. A beautiful vocal prayer, for example, is the invocation of your guardian angel, who has a great role to play in your redemption and mine. "Angel of God, my guardian dear . . ." Though this popular prayer has fixed words, you can always change them into a brief aspiration or call for help, for instance while traveling or walking alone in a questionable neighborhood. The Holy Rosary is a beautiful and powerful vocal prayer that goes right to the heart of the Mother of God because the Hail Mary was the greeting of the angel to her ("Hail, full of grace, the Lord is with thee") and the call to her vocation. All of the set vocal prayers come from the rich tradition of the Church. They can help you to come closer to God and, in turn, give Him to others.

But silent prayer is also important. Often in the Gospel we find Christ praying alone: before His public ministry, before choosing His Apostles, before His passion and death, and numerous other times. Even though He is God Himself, His human nature feels the need to be alone with His Father. Many times in our life we will feel the same need. Our prayer can simply be a prayer of presence by passing time silently looking at God in an adoration chapel where the Blessed Sacrament is exposed. Or we may choose to meditate on some text from the Bible or an inspiring spiritual book, and talk with God about that passage in our own words. We may choose to speak to Him personally about something that's bothering us or that we don't understand. In these kinds of prayer we can insistently repeat the petition of the blind man in the Gospel: "Master, let me receive my sight" (Mark 10:51).

At certain times we will have a joy or success to communicate to God, so we can make acts of thanksgiving. There will also be times of suffering and darkness, when our prayer may even come close to Jesus' own prayer on the Cross: "My God, my God, why have you forsaken me?" (Matt 27:46). Let's even learn to give thanks for these times of greater trial because then our prayer becomes even more redemptive—and co-redemptive.

The main thing is not to give up. We must remember that prayer, whether it be with others or more private, should always be a personal communication with God. The other day, I read in the news about a thirteen-year-old girl who sent or received twenty thousand text messages a week. Of course that seems excessive, but couldn't we have the same desire to communicate with God and send the Father, Son, and Holy Spirit more than twenty thousand messages a week? Or receive as many from them? Prayer means communication, and it is much more powerful than electronics.

One of God's complaints with the people of the Old Testament is that "this people . . . honor[s] me with their lips, while their hearts are far from me" (Isa 29:13). If we are going to be true co-redeemers, we must try to pray like Christ Himself, that is, from the heart. The *Catechism of the Catholic Church* describes the heart as "our hidden center, beyond the grasp of our reason and of others; only the Spirit of God can fathom the human heart and know it fully. The heart is the place of decision, deeper than our psychic drives. It is the place of truth, where we choose life or death" (*CCC* 2563). It is not easy to have such profound prayer always because we can suffer from all types of distractions and concerns, but it is certainly the most effective kind of prayer.

One does not have to have great feelings or emotions to pray from the heart. The main thing is to be very sincere and personal with God and to commit ourselves to live our lives in the way He wishes for us.

The Liberating Effect of Prayer

We said before that one of the characteristics of redemption is that it frees us from darkness and self-absorption. Good prayer does the same. It removes us from the trap of pride and self-pity and brings us into dialogue with God, who truly liberates us. Self-involvement can quickly put us into a dark world, where we are the victim of our own moods, fears, resentments, and sadness. All of those conditions can easily lead to sin and despair. To be enclosed in ourselves is similar to being in a dark and isolated room, refusing to let in God's sunshine or fresh air, or even other people's love.

Besides self-absorption, there are other enemies to prayer that we must overcome if we are to become true friends of Jesus Christ and to help others. One we can call *activity-ism*—the tendency to fill our day with mere activities: phone calls, computer messages, useless conversations, running around to different places. If we have no goal to our day, we will end up exhausted and disillusioned. But prayer and reflection give depth and quality to our day. We are not like haphazard autumn leaves blown into the gutter. For this reason, we should have a plan of prayer each day: a morning offering, as mentioned above, a time to be alone with God for several moments or more, short aspirations and reflections that will give our life direction.

Escapism is another enemy of prayer. Some individuals actually run from being alone with God. They try to fill up their day with other things that are not He. It's as if they're afraid of reflecting calmly for a while or of seeing the real truth about themselves. Thus, they try to escape in many ways: television, sports, gossip, computer games, parties, or worse. What they really need is the redemptive experience of prayer. A rich prayer life will "buy them back" from superficial things and put them into the heart of Christ, which is their only security in the end.

Pride is probably the worst enemy of prayer, for the proud person doesn't think she needs to pray. She thinks that she has it all together, that she is talented and organized, and that she doesn't have to ask anyone for anything. She is totally self-sufficient. Deep down, though she may not articulate it in this way, she doesn't think that she needs

God. And, therefore, she doesn't pray, or thinks it's a waste of time for her. If she's really blind, she may even dismiss prayer as something for the weak, the superstitious, or the unenlightened. Unless she becomes humble and sees the need to pray, she will end up totally disillusioned and frustrated with herself and others.

St. Teresa of Ávila was a great Carmelite mystic in the sixteenth century. Her writings, especially those about the power of prayer, have inspired many throughout the years. I conclude this section with one of her most dramatic statements about personal prayer and its great benefit for a soul: "The devil knows that he has lost a soul that perseveringly practices mental prayer."

Humility and Perseverance

Our Savior gave us many instructions on the way to pray. The first is to pray sincerely, from the heart, as we said before. "God, be merciful to me a sinner!" the tax-collector said from his heart in the Temple (Luke 18:13). His prayer was truly humble; he recognizes his littleness before God, and he is willing to convert. Humility and readiness to change our lives are two essential qualities of redemptive prayer.

Another quality is perseverance. Christ greatly praises consistency and insistence in prayer. "Ask, and it will be given to you; seek, and you will find; knock, and it will be opened to you" (Matt 7:7). He praises the relentless widow who kept knocking at the door of the unjust judge until she wears him out (see Luke 18:1–8). If our prayer is to be truly redemptive, we must literally bombard God with petitions:

for the protection of unborn children, for the conversion of hearts, for vocations, for world peace, for the physical and spiritual health of a loved one. Such persevering prayer is really a consequence of faith: we believe that there is a great and good God who listens to us and wants our good. And He has told us to keep petitioning Him, even *bothering* Him, until He's forced to give in!

Another aspect of good prayer is boldness. If we are truly children of God, if we are the objects of His special favor, let's ask Him for the moon and more! "Whatever you ask in prayer, believe that you receive it, and you will" (Mark 11:24). "All things are possible to him who believes" (Mark 9:23). The saints were quite adept at this kind of prayer. Imagine the boldness of St. Patrick's prayer when he returned to Ireland in order to convert the very people who had enslaved him. Imagine the boldness of St. Catherine's prayer when she went to Avignon in France to convince the pope to return to Rome. Imagine the boldness of St. Isaac Jogues' prayer as he entered a village of hostile Native Americans in order to speak to them of Christ and the Faith. Imagine your own boldness when you must speak to a group of friends about why consuming certain media would be bad for their souls.

When our prayer is constant, a great thing happens in our life. The Holy Spirit begins to fill us, more and more, with His gifts. Along with other graces, He gives us the wisdom to see both people and things in their true light; He gives us the counsel to make the right decision at the right time; He gives us the fortitude to keep on the right path despite the difficulties—from inside or outside; He gives us the good fear of offending God who loves us so much; He

gives us piety, or a tender desire to pray well and to participate in the Church's liturgy with devotion.

CHAPTER 5

Sanctifying Work

"A sower went out to sow." (Matt 13:3)

FOR MANY PEOPLE, WORK IS A CURSE. It is something they would rather avoid, do little of, or leave for other people. They complain frequently if they have to work even a little more than usual and are always waiting for their next vacation. But this is to misunderstand the real nature of human work and how it perfects us. Working well and conscientiously develops our minds, will, and physical powers. It gives glory to God, as Adam and Eve did with their work in the Garden of Paradise (see Gen 2:15). It contributes to the good of society if it is well done. In the words of St. Josemaría, "Professional work is also an apostolate, an opportunity to give ourselves to others, to reveal Christ to them and lead them to God the Father."[1]

We can truly say that work well done is a way of bringing God's own kingdom to the world.

The Gospel parables of the kingdom of God are very simple and persuasive lessons about how redemption works. Christ uses real-life examples to explain the mysterious working of grace in people's souls and in the world: it could

---

[1] St. Josemaría Escrivá, *Christ Is Passing By* (New York: Scepter Publishers, 1973), no. 49.

be a farmer sowing seed, a woman looking for a lost coin, a servant investing money with bankers. You might think that the Savior would give highly elevated or erudite examples to explain the workings of God's kingdom; but the vast majority of His teachings are drawn from the everyday experiences of ordinary men and women.

There is something redemptive, therefore, about ordinary work. Christ Himself chose to spend the largest part of His life on earth making a living like those around Him, working with His hands. He had to meet deadlines, we can be sure, and deal with unreasonable or cranky clients—even some who would not pay their bills. He had to overcome tiredness and tribulations in His job, like we do. As we said in the first chapter, He chose to be like us in everything except sin.

A text from the Second Vatican Council gives us a key insight concerning redemptive work: "By His incarnation the Son of God has united Himself in some fashion with every man. He worked with human hands, He thought with a human mind, acted by human choice and loved with a human heart."[2]

There is a powerful theological consequence to this truth. Everything that a divine Person does has consequences beyond the mere work itself; His actions resonate throughout time and eternity. We should keep in mind that the *whole life* of Christ was redemptive, including the smallest, most ordinary actions. All of His actions offered praise and atonement to God the Father, though His loving sacri-

---

[2]   Second Vatican Council, Pastoral Constitution on the Church in the Modern World *Gaudium et Spes* (December 7, 1965), §22.

fice was totally fulfilled and culminated on the Cross and in the Resurrection. If we connect our daily work with His, especially in the Sacrifice of the Mass, then our work can truly become a prayer, and, yes, it can also be redemptive. It is not only the priest's work, with his administration of the sacraments, preaching, and spiritual direction, that is redemptive. In union with Christ and His sacrifice, every person can give glory to God and sanctify himself and others through ordinary tasks. For this reason, something as simple as setting a table can be redemptive if done well and for the right intention—namely, for the love of God and others.[3]

In some way, sanctified work is also connected with the final coming of Christ in His kingdom and the restoration of mankind. Originally, work was not meant to be a curse or a frustrating experience; it was part of the perfection that Adam and Eve enjoyed in paradise (see Gen 2:15). They used their intelligence and other faculties to give form, order, and beauty to the Garden of Eden—thereby giving praise and glory to their Creator. Work was originally meant to perfect human beings and offer the world to God. It was also meant to help human beings to observe and appreciate God's wisdom, power, and goodness as reflected in His creation.

But the original sin of Adam and Eve, along with their descendants' own sins, have disfigured human work, and often have lowered it the level of greed, manipulation, and egotism. The Savior's humble work in Nazareth, and

---

[3] See Javier López and Ernst Burkhart, *Ordinary Life and Holiness in the Teaching of St. Josemaría: A Study in Spiritual Theology*, (New York: Scepter Publishers, 2017), 286–87.

throughout His life, restores the true meaning to human work. The Gospel tells us that "He has done all things well" (Mark 7:37). The quality of His work, and the love that He put into it, bought us back from the dominance of sin and the devil and placed us once again in God's favor.

Building His Kingdom

As a result, the work of Christ's disciples—done in the state of grace and in union with Christ Himself—will build up His kingdom on earth. Though His definitive kingdom will not come as a result of human progress or effort, sanctified human work disposes man and society for Christ's coming. Speaking of the fruits of human labor on earth, Vatican II's *Gaudium et Spes* states that "we will find them again, but freed of stain, burnished and transfigured, when Christ hands over to the Father: 'a kingdom eternal and universal'. . . . On this earth that Kingdom is already present in mystery. When the Lord returns it will be brought into full flower."[4]

This has many practical consequences. A physician who gives excellent care to his patients, not only with the best medical technology but with true charity and respect for their dignity, is preparing the world for Christ's final coming—for Christ the Divine Physician, who heals both bodies and souls. A woman who converts her house into a home by her generous and diligent effort is preparing her family and many future homes for the coming of Christ's own Family—for the Holy Trinity of the divine Persons, and

---

[4] Second Vatican Council, *Gaudium et Spes*, §39.

the Trinity on earth, Jesus, Mary, and Joseph. A janitor who gives excellent cleaning service in a building entrusted to him prefigures the purification that Christ will give for the entire human race—for the spotless Temple of God which Christ will establish forever.

Creativity and progress are part of sanctifying work as well. One of the positive contributions of the modern mentality to our history is that new and better methods of working can and should be developed. This involves using our human talents of inventiveness and experimentation. Persons who discover new things for the benefit of mankind—such as conserving energy, curing diseases, better methods of education—are like the servants in the Gospel who use their talents well. God praises them for their ingenuity and hard work (see Matt 25:21). The same applies to persons in ethical and philosophical endeavors. Indeed, the need to combine ethical insight with scientific research is one of the key challenges of our day.

The list of possibilities could go on. Any noble human work can be sanctified. If it is done well according to human standards of quality and excellence; if it is done with thoughtfulness and generosity (not simply for egotism or to make money); if it is done, above all, in union with Jesus of Nazareth and the Holy Sacrifice of the Mass, it can truly redeem the world. "Understand this well," St. Josemaría Escrivá, the founder of Opus Dei, once said, "There is something holy, something divine, hidden in the most ordinary situations, and it is up to each one of you to discover it. . . . No, my children! We cannot lead a double life. We cannot have a split personality if we want to be Christians. There is only one life, made of flesh and spirit. And it is that life which has to become, in both soul and body, holy and filled with God: we discover the invisible God in the most visible and material things."[5]

There are many ways that you can sanctify your work. First, as we said above, it has to be done well. We cannot please God with a poor or shoddy effort. An example from the Old Testament may help. In the time after the Jewish people returned from Babylon, the Temple was rebuilt and offerings were brought to it. But some of the people were "cheap" with God; instead of bringing young and strong sheep to offer, they would bring animals that were lame or sick (see Mal 1:13). The prophet Malachi severely chastised them for that: they were trying to cheat God but only cheated themselves. The message is clear for all of us. When we work, we should give God our best. Whatever we do, it should be done punctually, completely, and with attention to detail. It also helps to have a smile on our face.

Faith, Hope, and Charity

I remember a marvelous little book about sanctifying work written by one of the first priests of Opus Dei who went to England many years ago. In one section he speaks about the "three ways of sweeping a floor," which may not sound like a very transcendental topic, but it has a deep message. The first way of sweeping a floor, he said, was to do it grudgingly, as if it were beneath our dignity, and trying to finish it as

---

[5] St. Josemaría Escrivá, "Passionately Loving the World: Homily Given during Mass on the Campus of the University of Navarre, October 8, 1967," in *Conversations with Josemaría Escrivá* (New York: Scepter Publishing, 1968), 177.

soon as possible. The other way was to do it mechanically, like a robot—efficient, but without any particular intention or motivation. The third way was to sweep the floor thoroughly and well, for the love of God and of those dwelling in the house. Then he asked: which is the best way of sweeping the floor?

In the previous chapter we mentioned the importance of the morning offering, which can be renewed throughout your day. Another way of connecting your work with Christ is to carry a crucifix or rosary in your pocket or purse and use it to remember the purpose of your efforts. You could even place the crucifix on your desk or next to your laptop as a way to offer your actions generously to God.

Usually, we think of the virtues of faith, hope, and charity in the context of prayer or a religious setting. But they also have meaning in sanctifying our tasks. "Faith, hope, and charity will come into play in your professional work done for God."[6] It can certainly be said that we exercise faith in God's will when we report to work on time and try to do our best each day. We don't run away from our duties but recognize them as giving glory to God and making us more holy. Even the little things of our day can be offered with a generous spirit, which often requires a great faith.

We exercise the virtue of hope when we try to connect what we do with the good of all mankind, and the coming of God's kingdom. We may not see the results of our labors, but we have hope in their supernatural value. St. Paul has a mysterious passage in the Letter to the Romans that speaks of the Christians' transformation and liberation of the entire

[6] Escrivá, *Christ Is Passing By*, no. 49.

universe. "For creation waits with eager longing for the revealing of the sons of God . . . because the creation itself will be set free from its bondage to decay and obtain the glorious liberty of the children of God" (Rom 8:19, 21). Every task done with love and in the state of grace somehow liberates the world from sinfulness and decay. It connects human life with the hope of the Resurrection of Christ.

Charity is the greatest virtue of all, of course. But we mustn't think of it only in sentimental terms. It is the theological virtue that gives form and motivation to all the others. We have faith and hope within us because God loved us first and gave these virtues to us. In the same way love should form the mainspring of our daily work. "Do everything for love," writes St. Josemaría. "In that way there will be no little things: everything will be big."[7] When we work with charity, we participate more deeply in Christ's redemption, which of course was carried out because of His infinite love for us. It is like the leaven in the flour that raises the bread and makes it nutritious. For this reason, we should try to see our work as giving glory to God for His goodness and as reflecting that goodness in what we do—by the quality of our activity, by our thoughtfulness, and by our good humor and sacrifice for others.

Let's conclude by asking St. Joseph, who instructed Christ and worked at His side in the carpenter's shop, to help us to sanctify our daily tasks and connect them with the redemption of society. Certainly his intercession has great power in heaven with Christ. He can win for us the

---

[7]   St. Josemaría Escrivá, *The Way* (New York: Scepter Publishers, 1992), no. 813.

graces that we need to transform the world from within, particularly through the exercise of faith, hope, and love in our daily activities.

CHAPTER 6

Matrimony as Co-Redemption

The Calling to Love and Be Loved

WITHIN OUR GENERAL VOCATION to be in the Church and share in Christ's redemptive mission, God has a special plan for our life. Since God created us in His image and likeness, we each have a deep desire to love and be loved, just as the three Persons of the Holy Trinity share an infinite life of knowledge and love, which includes the gift of Themselves to one another.

Every man and woman needs to find someone to fulfill this deep longing of the human heart placed in us by our Creator. Some individuals are called to give themselves completely to God in a life of celibacy. They are called to renounce their right to marry and have children for the sake of a higher calling: to serve God either as religious or priests, or as dedicated laypeople who live individually or in community. These people imitate most closely the life of Christ and His Apostles, who gave up everything to follow Him and to give witness to His kingdom, either in this world or in the next. They also imitate the life and vocation of Mary, Mother of Christ, who remained a virgin all of her life in complete service to God's unique plan for her.

But most men and women are called to find God and fulfillment in this life through close and intimate contact with a partner of the opposite sex. Such was God's original plan for the human race as we see in the persons of Adam and Eve. They were called to be mutually complementary, and to find happiness together in the Garden of Eden. As Adam said of Eve when he first saw her: "This at last is bone of my bones and flesh of my flesh" (Gen 2:23). Man and woman were thus created equal in dignity and were united to one another with very deep bonds. They were called to be intimate with one another in "one flesh," signifying the covenant of love between them.

This was God's original plan, as Christ would later tell the Pharisees. God's plan from the beginning was that the union of marriage would be indissoluble—that no one has the power to break it (see Matt 19:6). He also intended that this union should be fruitful and that the human race should multiply and "fill the earth" (Gen 1:28). In these two ways, openness to mutual love-giving and openness to children, man and woman would find happiness together on this earth. They were also meant to help and strengthen each other through their specific natural qualities, as male and female.

Of course, we know that Adam and Eve sinned gravely by disobedience to God, having been tempted by the devil, and as a result, their union lost its integrity and innocence. After sin they began to view each other lustfully and with shame. There would also be mutual accusations and selfish attitudes, with conflicting goals and desires. Human work would become toilsome, and childbearing would come with discomfort and pain.

But all was not lost. Before they were expelled from paradise, God gave them a great hope: that one of their descendants would crush the head of the evil one who had perverted them (see Gen 3:15). This saving grace would come to the world through a virgin, a daughter of Eve but conceived without sin; by the power of the Holy Spirit, she would bring a Redeemer to the fallen race of all mankind. He was to be the victorious descendant of Adam and Eve who would deliver the human race from sin and death. And it is in close connection with Him and the sacrament which He would institute that a man and woman can truly participate in the mystery of redemption.

Sanctifying the Family

The first thing to remember is that Christ Himself, the Redeemer of all mankind, wanted to grow up in a family. He could have appeared on earth as a grown man doing miracles, forming His Apostles and beginning the Church. But no, He wanted to be like us in everything: He spent nine months in His mother's womb as a pre-born child; He was a toddler learning how to walk and to speak His first words; He was subject to the authority of a man and a woman (Joseph and Mary). He also must have done many chores and daily tasks in that little home in Nazareth where He grew up.

In Saint Joseph, all fathers have a model of courage and common sense, as this holy man was chosen to protect and lead Mary and her child, and to provide for them both materially and personally. In Mary all mothers have their model of faith and continuous care for their families, as she cooperated most completely with God's will for her as a wife and mother, who both loved and supported her husband and child always. And of course in the Christ child all children have their model of the love and respect which they owe to their parents; for He chose to be subject to a father and a mother, and to obey them in the many details of daily life, even though they were mere creatures, and He was God himself. The above facts have great repercussions for our theme of co-redemption. All families, as long as they are monogamous like the Holy Family, give glory to God for what they are, and they can bring grace and salvation to the human race. Pregnancy, childbirth, and the raising of children all have powerful repercussions if united to Christ and the Holy Family of Nazareth.

What first constitutes a human family is the bond between husband and wife, which Pope St. John Paul II described as the "first communion" in a family.[1] It is a life of mutual support and encouragement that is sustained by affection and commitment to one another. Such is the nature of marriage on a natural level.

But through the Sacrament of Matrimony, that life is enhanced and uplifted; through the comings and goings, the ups and downs of daily life, husband and wife forge a path to heaven together, though God will do most of the work. Each must find the way to forgive, to be generous, to go forward together—taking into account one another's flaws and weaknesses. The husband who has to overcome his tiredness upon returning home in order to be fully present with his wife and children and to give himself to them; the wife who overcomes her anxieties and frustrations and

---

[1] See Pope St. John Paul II, Post-Synodal Apostolic Exhortation on the Role of the Christian Family in the Modern World *Familiaris Consortio* (November 22, 1981), §19.

presents a welcoming smile for her husband and who has kept the home clean and joyful for him: this is solid cooperation with Christ and real co-redemption, without the need to call it as such. "For a Christian marriage is not just a social institution, much less a mere remedy for human weakness. It is a real supernatural calling. A great sacrament, in Christ and in the Church."[2]

Couples sanctify their marriage when they pray for one another, when they work together as loving partners toward the same goal. (For most this includes the raising of children, but couples without children can also work together in a marvelous way to sanctify their relationship and do good for those around them.) For couples with children, love and a common goal continue when children grow up and leave the home. These are special years in which their love and unity can become stronger; now they can concentrate more on each other, and their companionship can become more unique and excellent as they care for each other in old age. They can fulfill to the end their marriage vow and their sacramental covenant: *for better, for worse, for richer, for poorer, in sickness and in health, to love and to cherish until death do us part.*

Ultimately, a sanctified marriage means fidelity. It is not only sexual fidelity but personal and spiritual fidelity to that person who is on the same path to God. Such fidelity is truly co-redemptive. Both husband and wife together discover Christ in their relationship, even through pain and misunderstandings, and their mutual love is a reflection of Christ's own love for His Body, the Church.

---

[2]   St. Josemaría Escrivá, *Christ Is Passing By* (New York: Scepter Publishers, 1973), no. 23.

But marriage is not only for the fulfillment of the married couple. A couple who is truly in love and working to enhance their love each day can be a tremendous inspiration to other couples and to their children. They can see the beauty and fruitfulness of the couple's lives and may wish to imitate it. Even seeing a large family with three or more children waiting in line somewhere or occupying a pew in church can be quite moving. No words need be spoken in these moments; the parents and children themselves are giving witness to the value of familial love and its beauty.

Couples who really love one another will not be in "their own worlds." Since they are one, in both body and in spirit, they should be in constant communication. This doesn't mean that they always have to be talking, rather that they are always united and moving in the same direction even without words—though occasionally there may be disagreements and quarrels. If they have the same general goal of giving glory to God and finding Christ in their marriage, they will certainly assist Him in His redemption.

Part of the unity of marriage is the capacity to dream together: about the family they will have, professional goals, the friends they will make, or the travels they will do together. But their greatest dream should always be based on Christ's Gospel message: how they can become saints together and how they can further His kingdom on earth. Of course, their most wonderful and all-encompassing dream should be their mutual desire to spend eternity together adoring God. For even though in heaven the blessed "neither marry nor are given in marriage" (Matt 22:30), there is surely a countless multitude of couples enjoying God together because they brought Him into their relationship on earth.

The Role of Marital Intimacy

All aspects of marital love can become redemptive if they are carried out according to God's eternal plan. As we saw earlier, God's plan for man and woman was for them to be "one flesh" (Gen 2:24) and to be partners for one another, equal in dignity. Every time a couple engages in marital intimacy, God is honored and praised, as long as the act is done according to God's plan of love and goodness. For this reason, contraceptive or lustful acts are not pleasing to God since they violate His plan for life and love between husband and wife. In the words of Pope John Paul II, contraceptive acts are a "falsification of the inner truth of conjugal love"[3] because they do not represent the complete gift of self that should exist between spouses.

Looking at it from a higher perspective, we can affirm that the world itself is a gift of the Blessed Trinity to humans, who were made in God's image and likeness and who are also persons as the Father, the Son, and the Holy Spirit are Persons. When man and woman love one another in a way open to both love and life, they are being co-creators and thus accompany God in His plan. God loved the human race from the beginning and wants them to populate the earth. "Be fruitful and multiply" (Gen 1:28), He told the first human couple. By sharing their love and by engendering children, they are giving glory to God Who is Life itself, and thus they open the way for His redemptive action to billions of human beings throughout history.

---

[3]   Pope St. John Paul II, *Familiaris Consortio*, §32, no. 4.

Having and Raising Children

A major part of God's redemptive plan for marriage is the having and raising of children. This is not meant to be simply a biological product of human love between male and female but the creation of a human person with an immortal soul, made in God's image and likeness. Every child in God's eyes is unique and has the right to be protected and loved so that he or she will grow up to live as God's son or daughter.

For this reason, a Christian couple should be open to having children and will be grateful for the life or lives entrusted to them. They also recognize that each child does not belong to them but to the one who created him or her. This is part of the couple's vocation to marriage, and if they do a conscientious job of both loving and forming their children, they will help to bring Christ's redemption to the world. That husband and wife really are co-redeemers of their children in addition to being parents.

Both father and mother will fulfill this responsibility in different ways. Mothers supply the love and warmth needed in every home; fathers supply the material means and personal leadership to go forward. This doesn't mean that fathers give no love or warmth to the family, or that mothers give no leadership or material support. Probably each of them will need to supply a bit of both throughout life; for both dads and moms give moral and spiritual guidance to their children, as well as material support, but in different ways. In addition, boys need their mothers, and girls need their fathers in order to grow in a balanced and fully human way and to be happy in their adult lives. Many psychological and social studies have corroborated this. There is no substitute for attentive love and guidance provided to a child in a stable home by a father and a mother who are faithful to one another.

As a result, good parents will always find time to accompany their children in their journeys throughout life— especially in their younger years—by conversing with them, by teaching them, by having fun with them, by correcting and encouraging them whenever needed. And of course, by praying with them. "What a son or daughter looks for in a father or mother is not only a certain amount of knowledge or some more or less effective advice, but primarily something more important: a proof of the value and meaning of life."[4] Such is the greatest gift that parents can give, though they may be limited socially or economically. The key goal is to give children *a proof of the value and meaning of life*— an example by which children can live lives of holiness. It should be something visibly shown by the father and mother and not simply be a lecture or explanation of morality or religion.

As we look at the world today, we see the disturbing situation of millions of people who don't see the meaning or purpose of human life aside from simple survival or individual accomplishments. It is distressing to see a large number of young people today, many of them with children, who describe themselves as "nones"; when asked about their religion or belief, they simply answer, "None." They have no religious belief or affiliation and apparently don't see the need for it. The cultural context and subsoil for this development is a kind of pervasive relativism, that is, the notion

---

[4] Escrivá, *Christ Is Passing By*, no. 28.

that there are no real standards of right or wrong in life and that individuals "create their own truth" by their own ideas or personal choices.

In such a world, obviously, Christian parents have a powerful role to play. They must form and inform their children about God and His plan for the human race, which includes the commandments and the moral law, the life of prayer and human virtues, the proper use of technology, and a real care for other people and their needs. Recall what Christ said to His Apostles, and by extension to all of His followers throughout time: "You are the light of the world. . . . Let your light so shine before men" (Matt 5:14, 16).

We can truly affirm that couples who raise their children in this way are participating in Christ's redemption. They are engendering and forming men and women who will not only be good and loyal citizens of our country but will also become saints. And each of their children in turn can become a co-redeemer as well, whether they marry or remain single, whether they have a college degree or not, in whatever walk of life they choose. One can simply appreciate the multiplying effect on society such children will have as they grow and meet other people. And it began with the prayer, training, and good example they received from their parents.

Such parenting is also the seedbed for vocations, that is, for their children's response to the calling that God has for each of them. If children are formed to be generous with God and others and to appreciate virtue and self-sacrifice, they will be much more open to a vocation later in life, not only to marriage but to a complete gift of self to God and the Church: the gift of celibacy. This gift can do so much good in the world, as it has always done, whether in the religious life or priesthood or in complete dedication to God as a lay-person in society.

A most important task of parents is to raise their children in the spirit of freedom. This word is so often abused and misunderstood in our society today—everyone wants to be free, but often this is meant in a selfish and self-destructive way.

Real freedom, as Pope St. John Paul II teaches us, "consists not in doing what we like, but in having the right to do what we ought."[5] This is the freedom that truly liberates a person from the tyranny of selfishness and deception. The well-formed child not only knows what is right and wrong but has the virtue and willpower to choose what is good and to reject what is bad—not because he is forced to do so by his parents or threatened by others but because he himself desires to do what is good. There can be nothing so heartening to good parents as when they ask their daughter to stop watching an inappropriate movie and she does so willingly and right away; or even better, when she chooses to watch only good movies in the first place. The same applies to a son who voluntarily avoids violent, immoral, or immodest video games.

It is a great manifestation of freedom when a child does his chores at home, prays and goes to church, takes care of his younger siblings, and does his homework not because he is forced to do so but because he sees that these things are good and freely wants to do so. Parents who raise children

---

[5] Pope St. John Paul II, "Homily of His Holiness John Paul II," (Oriole Park at Camden Yards, Baltimore, MD, October 8, 1995), §7, https://www.vatican.va/content/john-paul-ii/en/homilies/1995/documents/hf_jp-ii_hom_19951008_baltimore.html.

in this way have really taught them to be free and not to be victims of their own whims or what society pushes on them. They have cooperated with the grace of Christ. They have become co-redeemers of their children by teaching them the meaning of real freedom.

But let's return for a moment to our previous consideration: having children in the first place. Oftentimes couples face opposition from friends and relatives for having more than two or three children. It takes courage and a belief in God's plan to be open to as many children as He wants to send, without recourse to contraception or abortion. The pregnancies of some women can be very painful, even dangerous, yet they desire to bring another life into the world. Or a father may find it difficult to find another job in order to support a new child, but he is willing to make heroic sacrifices to do so. Such a couple has real faith and brings a tremendous good in the world.

I remember hearing the story of a couple who lived in a big city in the U.S. The wife was having a difficult pregnancy, and was being treated by a gynecologist at a prestigious hospital, who discovered a serious genetic defect in the fetus. He encouraged her to terminate the pregnancy, saying that if the baby were born alive, he would live only a short time. Both husband and wife, believing in the value of every human life, refused. The wife even wanted to change physicians, but the husband insisted that they keep the same one since he was a top professional. When the baby was born, the husband baptized him immediately. By that time, many friends and members of the hospital staff had heard about the case and had gathered at the couple's room. A priest was called in to administer the Sacrament of Confirmation, which gave the child even more grace and the gifts of the Holy Spirit. Shortly afterward, the baby died, and a group photograph was taken next to the child's bed—a photo that included the doctor who had recommended the abortion. He had been deeply moved by the entire event. Such is the power of co-redemption: it not only involved the couple and their child but the souls of many others as well.

Grandparents can play a great part in the formation and education of children. Parents nowadays face many constraints, such as the need for both father and mother to work or other commitments (some of their own disordered choosing) that take them away from their children. In some cases, they ask the grandparents to babysit their grandchildren during the day rather than sending them to a daycare center. Even more importantly, many young people today are not giving their children a religious education; here grandparents have an essential role. They may have to provide a basic catechesis to their grandchildren on the faith or bring them to church on Sundays if the parents don't take them. Of course, this is a delicate issue because parents have the primary role of catechizing their children; but if they are neglectful, grandparents (and of course godparents) can and should intervene for the good of the children. By praying *for* and *with* grandchildren and godchildren, they supplement what they are not receiving at home.

Grandparents can be a great support even in little things relating to God and religion, such as saying simple prayers with the children or taking them for a visit to the Blessed Sacrament. Oftentimes, telling stories about their own youth and marriage can open children's eyes to God's providence working in the history of their own family. They can give them a most valuable perspective: that they are part of a home and have a heritage with continuity and meaning. They can also show how God draws good from tough and painful situations, such as financial stress or physical or psychological illness.

Grandparents have the privilege of giving wise and timely advice to their own daughters and sons—if the parents are humble enough to receive it and still value the counsel of their parents, who have more experience of life and who have raised children of their own.

In all cases, we can speak of the *vocation* of grandparents to assist and supplement a family's life, especially in areas the parents of their grandchildren are not covering. This is a most valuable way of participating in Christ's redemption of their family in their later years.

CHAPTER 7

Giving Witness

"And he said to them, 'What is this conversation
which you are holding with each other as you walk?'
And they stood still, looking sad." (Luke 24:17)

DO YOU REMEMBER THIS EVENT IN THE GOSPEL? Two
disciples of Christ, Cleopas and a friend, were leaving the
scene in Jerusalem on the morning of the first Easter Sunday.
The events that had occurred in the previous days were too
much for them: the false trial of Christ, His condemnation
by Pilate, the bloody Crucifixion, the Apostles abandoning
the scene, and, finally, some of the women disciples appear-
ing just that morning and claiming that angels had told
them that He was alive. With all of this behind them, we
can understand why they would look confused and sad.

But then, after asking them what had happened and
why they were sad, the traveler accompanying them started
to explain how it all had to come to pass according to Scripture. "Was it not necessary that the Christ should suffer
these things and enter into his glory? And beginning with
Moses and all the prophets, he interpreted to them in
all the Scriptures the things concerning himself" (Luke
24:26–27). Christ proved Himself to be not a lone traveler
but their friend and their Savior. His words enlightened
their minds and gave new purpose and meaning to their

lives. "Did not our hearts burn within us while he talked to on the road, while he opened to us the Scriptures?" (Luke 24:32).

A follower of Christ, in whatever century, should have the same concern and zeal for his friends. It should hurt us to see people sad and confused. And even if they appear to be happy, it can often happen that if you scratch the surface a bit, you will find underneath a deep sadness or pessimism about themselves and the world. Someone might say that their lives have *no story*. Life is just one event after another, whether those events are painful, pleasurable, or non-descript. If once they had an ideal, it has disappeared, and they are just waiting out the years of their life to go they know not where.

Each of us through Baptism has been configured to Christ in His role as prophet, king, and priest. A good part of our prophetic mission is to give witness to the truth of Christ and His Church. We cannot lead isolated lives, indifferent to others and their situation. We, too, like the first disciples, must hear Our Lord telling us: "Go therefore and make disciples of all nations" (Matt 28:19). Redemption in great part means giving light to others, for the two strongest desires in the human soul are for truth and for love. If these two are not fulfilled, people will be ever restless and discontent.

Identifying the Obstacles

Besides atheism and agnosticism, there are three main "isms" that afflict people today, shutting them in a kind of tunnel. They are predominant philosophies or mindsets that ultimately deny that man has a spiritual soul and a supernatural destiny. Though they purport to affirm man, they really do just the opposite: these thought systems violate basic human dignity, leading men and women into a kind of slavery. One of them is materialism, the lifestyle that ignores or rejects the fact that we are made in the image and likeness of God and therefore have an intellect and free will. People think that they are enjoying the "good life" because they are measuring it in very narrow terms—convenience, money, pleasures. But none of these material things can free them from the prison of themselves. If we are Christ's apostles we will try, through our words and actions, to show people the real truth about human existence and the way to authentic happiness.

The second "ism" that is an enemy of modern people is relativism. This is the philosophy—or better, the non-philosophy (for there is no meaningful thought behind it)—that there is no right or wrong, and that we cannot judge the morality of human actions. It claims that everyone sees things from his or her point of view, so everyone is really "right," no matter what they do. Relativism disguises itself as sophistication and "openness" but, in the end, it brings only chaos to people's lives.

I remember the humorous story of an announcement that the captain of a passenger jet made before takeoff. "Hi folks," he said over the speaker, "the co-pilot and I have not come to an agreement on whether the left engine of this aircraft is working or not. But since neither of us wants to impose his opinion on the other, we are going to take off anyhow. I hope you enjoy your flight, and thanks again for flying with us today."

The question raises itself. How can a society survive

if there is no basic agreement on the value of human life, marriage, and moral responsibility? How can any nation or people go forward without basic principles and common goals? For instance, one of the driving arguments today for promoting certain movements in this country, including gay marriage, is that one must be tolerant and open-minded. If you oppose gay marriage for moral reasons, or because it would eventually undermine the authentic marriage of a man and a woman, you can be called intolerant or homophobic. Political correctness has substituted basic morals, especially in college settings. And so, people are afraid to say or do anything for fear of offending someone. The gay agenda is perfectly logical in a way: If there is no such thing as human nature, if people and the world are constantly evolving, why defend anything, including marriage? And if there is no human nature, there is no such thing as sin or virtue either; they don't make sense.

True, there may be laws prohibiting certain things, or certain actions are deemed unacceptable, but nobody gives any consistent or deep reason for such laws and evaluations; they are seen to be mere social necessities. Everything depends on circumstances and human opinions. If one does claim to know certain moral truths, he or she can easily be branded a "religious fanatic" or as unwilling to listen to all sides of the question. Relativism permits dishonesty, sexual immorality, abortion, even blasphemy. It also leads to a complete skepticism about God and religion and makes it easy to believe that "might makes right" and "the end justifies the means."

For all of these reasons, Pope Benedict XVI rightfully identified relativism as a *dictatorship* that holds power over a great part of the Western world today, especially Europe and the United States.

The third great enslaver of people today is eroticism, which exaggerates and distorts the meaning of sexual pleasure. As a result, many couples contracept in their marriages, violating the nature of their bodies and their intimacy so as to avoid the coming of new life. Many others are addicted to sexual experiences on the internet or similar electronic media, even to the point of neglecting their work and their families. Premarital sex is rampant on college campuses, which really degrades the young man and woman involved in these actions; rather than a complete gift of self within marriage, it changes the sexual act into something selfish and transitory. Many movies and TV shows include explicit sexual scenes in order to gain more money or popularity for their producers.

Ultimately, all of these effects of eroticism are a symptom of something much more serious, which is related to materialism and relativism: the view that men and women are only animals with no interior standards of right or wrong and no spiritual principle or soul within them.

The Truth Will Make You Free

In the face of all this, a man or woman of God needs to be courageous, and like the early Christians, they must try to change and redeem the pagan world. Followers of Christ must realize that they have something within them that is stronger than the materialism that enslaves many men and women around them. At times, even without their desiring it, their attitudes and actions will be a slap in the face of others: "My girlfriend and I are waiting for marriage to have sexual relations." "That business deal is morally wrong; we shouldn't do it." "This movie is no good; let's leave." "We should not just look the other way; we should do something to help the poor people in our neighborhood." These are examples of redemptive attitudes. They might produce scorn; we may lose friends, we may even be marginalized or attacked—but all of them connect us with Christ the Light of the world.

Of course, not all witnessing needs to be confrontational. Oftentimes, we will be able to do things in a natural and pleasant way that draws attention to our beliefs and can even gently persuade others. I remember the story of a woman at work who refused to gossip and deftly tried to turn the conversation away from speaking badly about others. She would simply try to bring up good things about the person in question or try to get others to understand that person's situation better. She would not add to the gossip but tried to channel office conversations in a more positive direction. Once she even said, "Let's pray for her; it sounds like she really needs help." By doing this patiently, day after day, she managed to change the entire tone of lunch-hour conversations. If for no other reason, people guarded their tongues because they respected her and didn't want to offend her; they knew that she was uncomfortable with gossip and negative commentaries.

This is an example of co-redemptive witnessing. She did not give a talk or lecture about charity but simply lived it, and others got the point. The same approach can be used in so many other situations—in the type of media you consume, in the quality and honesty of your work, in the way you comport yourself on a date, in the good humor and openness that you have toward family and children.

At times, however, we will be able to speak more directly about truth and ideals. It could happen that one of your Catholic friends has not been to Confession for a long time. The moment could be ripe for a personal conversation with him about the sacraments of the Church and how they bring us closer to God. You could even use your own experience as an example, namely, how a good and sincere confession really helped you to change your life. Or it could be that one of your coworkers is somewhat prejudiced toward a certain group of people; try to find a good moment to speak to him about some positive experience that you had with these individuals, and perhaps even give him a pertinent writing on social justice and charity from one of the popes.

In social situations certain people—including Catholics—often feel free to criticize the Catholic Church and even dissent from her teachings on faith or morals. As we mentioned in the section on the Church, at those moments we must have the courage to give witness, in a clear and charitable way, to her authentic teachings. If an argument ensues, the best thing is to pray and, at the right moment, give the dissenting person a good document of the Church to read that clearly addresses his or her problems. You could even refer them to a good website where you know that the Church's teachings are clearly elucidated and defended.

Courage and Responsibility

It is common to feel quite small and insignificant compared to all the problems and wrong attitudes around us. We could even think that the whole world is in the devil's power and there is nothing we can do. At those moments we must hear the Redeemer telling us: "Be of good cheer, I have overcome the world" (John 16:33), and "You have sorrow now, but I will see you again and your hearts will rejoice, and no one will take your joy from you" (John 16:22). Just like the first Apostles, we know that we have Christ's power working in us and through us. Throughout their lives, the Apostles must have always remembered the great miracle of the loaves and the fishes: a few loaves and fishes were enough to feed a huge crowd of men and women (see Mark 6:35–44).

I once read a biblical commentator who speculated about two ways that this miracle could have been done: Christ could have suddenly made a huge pile of bread and fish appear, and the disciples simply drew from it to give to the people; or the disciples, moved by faith, could have just started to distribute the few loaves and fishes that they had to the crowds, but, somehow, they always had enough in their baskets to feed the multitudes. I personally think it happened in this latter way. It often seems that the true followers of Christ are very few and working with hardly anything, yet Christ's power works through them, and they end up feeding thousands of people because of Him.

This applies to both priests and laypeople. Sometimes certain individuals say that it is the priests and the bishops or the consecrated religious who bring grace and redemption to the world. They forget that all the baptized faithful have the mission to bring Christ's truth to the world. "The laity derive the right and duty to the apostolate from their union with Christ the head; incorporated into Christ's Mystical Body through Baptism and strengthened by the power of the Holy Spirit through Confirmation, they are assigned to the apostolate by the Lord Himself."[1]

The lay faithful, drawing their strength from Christ in prayer and the Eucharist, can reach many places where priests and religious could never reach: the intimacy of the home, the workings of a factory or business, the football or soccer field, the scientific laboratory or operating room.

In other words, the chance for giving witness to Christ's truth and love is immense. Without in any way bragging or giving into egotism, the baptized faithful can fulfill to the letter those Gospel words: "Let your light so shine before men, that they may see your good works and give glory to your Father who is in heaven" (Matt 5:16). One of the greatest phenomena in the early Church was the large number of people, especially young men and women, who committed themselves to a life of celibacy for the sake of loving God and spreading His kingdom on earth.[2] They came from all classes of society and lived either with their families, by themselves, or with others who had the same dedication. Their witness was particularly powerful in that pagan world, where many pursued only selfish goals for their lives, as we read in the works of St. Justin Martyr (around AD 150).[3] In particular, their commitment showed that loving God above all things and following Christ's own

---

[1] Second Vatican Council, Decree on the Apostolate of the Laity *Apostolicam Actuositatem* (November 18, 1965), §3.

[2] See Athenagoras of Athens, "Apology to Marcus Aurelius," in *Ancient Christian Authors* (London: The Newman Press, 1956), 74.

[3] See St. Justin Martyr, "Apology to the Emperor Antininus Pius," in *Ancient Christian Martyrs* (Mahwah, NJ: Paulist Press, 1997), nos. 15, 29 (p. 32); Michael Giesler, "Celibacy in the First Two Centuries," *Homiletic and Pastoral Review* (January 2009).

life of celibacy was not only a beautiful thing to do; it was a transforming way of life.

Giving witness to Christ will give us big hearts and noble ideals. We will not give into the train of thought that says there's nothing we can do or that "this is just the way things are." Oftentimes that is the language of laziness and cowardice. If we have minds and hearts modeled on Christ and the Apostles, we will *want* to have many friends, and through our friendships we will change the world. Pope Benedict XVI said something very similar to youth in Australia in 2008: "Dear young people, . . . what will *you* leave to the next generation? Are you building your lives on firm foundations, building something that will endure? Are you living your lives in a way that opens up space for the Spirit in the midst of a world that wants to forget God, or even rejects him . . . ?"[4] Let's therefore take the Pope's challenge and feel the responsibility of being co-redeemers—with family members and friends, with fellow Catholics, with people of all religions and backgrounds.

We should also feel responsible for our nation. It is not simply in the hands of elected officials or politicians; it is very much in *our* hands. For this reason, we should pray every day for the big issues facing our country: the protection of innocent human life at all stages, the defense and promotion of marriage as the union between a man and a woman, world peace, education in virtue, and care for the environment. Giving witness to the teachings of Christ and the Church in

---

[4] Pope Benedict XVI, "Address of His Holiness," (World Youth Day Vigil, July, 2008), https://www.vatican.va/content/benedict-xvi/en/homilies/2008/documents/hf_ben-xvi_hom_20080720_xxiii-wyd.html.

all of these areas can bring healing to our country. At times this could mean sending good messages to your friends on social media; or you could join a pro-life initiative like 40 Days for Life. It certainly means voting intelligently, with sound moral criteria, for the best candidate. It could even mean running for public office ourselves as a positive way to influence for the common good of our society.

So often, in the entire question of apostolic work and giving witness to God in the world, fear and human respects can deter us. This weakness prevents us from acting and speaking as Christ wants us to. It is easy to just "blend in" or "not make waves." We should not give into timidity. If we truly love Christ and His message, we will give witness to Him bravely and generously.

"Holy father keep them in your name, which you have given me, that they may be one, even as we are one" (John 17:11). Jesus Christ was the greatest Lover of all time. People who love want union with their beloved, and Christ wants this in a personal and deep way with every man and woman that ever lived or will live. For this reason He came to the world, was born in a poor stable in Bethlehem, performed miracles, died on the Cross, and rose again. For this reason He established a Church that would transmit His truth and love throughout the centuries—and yes, reach every man and woman who would ever live.

The biggest desire of His heart was, and *is*, to bring people to His Father in the love of the Holy Spirit. "Go therefore and make disciples of all nations," He told His Apostles, "baptizing them in the name of the Father and of the Son and of the Holy Spirit" (Matt 28:19). You and I have been chosen by Him to continue this mission. In many ways it's a "mission impossible." It involves prayer, pain, joy, and hard work. But the rewards are great, both now and afterward. "So every one who acknowledges me before men, I also will acknowledge before my Father who is in heaven" (Matt 10:32).

Let's ask Christ for a perfect love so that we can be His lips, hands, and feet in this confused world, so deeply in need of the truth, yet so constantly running from it.

CHAPTER 8

Co-Redemptive Friendship

The Meaning of Human Friendship

THE MYSTERY OF CO-REDEMPTION is based on deep and personal friendship with Jesus Christ. He is our greatest friend first of all by redeeming us. And as a result of knowing and loving Him, we bring Him to others. Or, as another way of saying it, Christ our friend *works in us to bring others to His friendship.*

Our Lord was the best of friends not only to His disciples but to all of those around Him. We see this constantly in the Gospel. He befriends the Samaritan woman who needed so much help (see John 4:7–30); He loves staying at the house of Lazarus, Martha, and Mary in Bethany, where He found family warmth and sincere conversation which He cherished so much (see John 11:5); He accompanies the two disciples who were leaving Jerusalem, about to give up their belief in Him, and He strengthens and encourages them (see Luke 24:32).

In the end, friendship is the message of His life since He came to the world to welcome all men and women into His family—the Father, Himself, and the Holy Spirit—and to bring all people to eternal happiness through His Church, His Mystical Body on earth, which extends His truth and love throughout the centuries. Real friendship always leads to the sharing of the good with the other; Christ does this during His entire life on earth and beyond. By coming to the world, He shares His charity and His humanity with us in a complete way, as He actually became one of us, with a body and soul like ours. And because He is fully God and fully man at the same time, He enables us to find grace and divine meaning in all human activities.

The true friend, by sharing his life and ideas with another, gives his friend a certain new meaning and joy, which can often bring him out of loneliness or sadness. Christ, who is the perfect friend, draws all of us out of sadness and confusion. We don't really know ourselves until we discover Christ. For this reason, the Second Vatican Council states that He fully reveals man to himself.[1] He shows how life can be restored and elevated in us, especially in those things that have been lost or disfigured by sin. His friendship brings us grace and hope, leading us to a complete union with Himself and His Father. And He does all of this by becoming one of us completely, body, soul, mind, and heart. Remember this magnificent quote from the Second Vatican Council: "For, by His Incarnation, He, the Son of God, in a certain way united Himself with each man. He worked with human hands, He thought with a human mind, He acted with a human will, and with a human heart He loved."[2]

Ultimately, Christ's friendship with us culminated on the Cross, where He shed His blood and died for us. This was the supreme gift of friendship because it forgave all of our sins and opened the gate of eternal life to us. "Greater

---

[1] Second Vatican Council, *Gaudium et Spes*, §22.
[2] Second Vatican Council, *Gaudium et Spes*, §22.

love has no man than this, that a man lay down his life for his friends. . . . but I have called you friends, for all that I have heard from my Father I have made known to you" (John 15:13, 15).

We, too, in a participatory but real way, can become co-redeemers as we work with Christ the great Friend and help our companions to come closer to Him. We, too, can bring truth and joy to them, removing the darkness and sadness that life often brings and sharing with them the path to personal fulfillment and eternal happiness. The Old Testament states that "a faithful friend is a sturdy shelter: he that has found one has found a treasure" (Sirach 6:14).

All human persons have the basic need of relating to another person. Since human beings are created in the image and likeness of God Himself, and God is one Being in three Persons Who know and love each other, our own person needs to reach out and find others in order to be fulfilled. Marriage itself, we have seen, is a kind of friendship, very unique and powerful, between a man and a woman; it consists of a partnership throughout life with a common goal. It ultimately involves the sharing of the good between husband and wife, parents and children.

But friendship is not limited to the immediate family. Parents and children need to have friends outside of the home who will provide experiences and insights that a single family cannot give. God's truth and goodness are spread throughout the world and are manifested in different individuals with different life experiences; no two human beings are the same. Friendship with others enriches and enhances a man's personality since it allows him to get out of himself both by learning from and giving to another.

Friendship is a relationship that can grow very quickly or come about little by little. Normally, for authentic friendship to form there has to be a longer contact between two persons who get to know each other gradually: their family history; their talents, virtues, and weaknesses; their goals in life. Slowly a bond develops. At other times, people seem to be "made for each other," and companionship develops very quickly. But the end result of both of these is a meeting of the mind and will that unites two people so that they enjoy and benefit from each other's company.

Good friends have similar views in sports, technology, entertainment, and philosophy of life, though at times they may differ in some things. They also have a certain equality of condition; each learns from the other, and each benefits from the other. It is not the same as the master-disciple relationship, the teacher-student relationship, or even the parent-child relationship (though real friendship can develop in each one of these). In a word, there is mutual freedom and real give-and-take in true friendships.

Real friendship involves the sharing of deeper thoughts and feelings. With someone we trust, we can even share without fear things that make us vulnerable. We know that our friend loves us and will not think less of us if we are honest with him or her. Nor will they gossip or speak badly about us. With a mere acquaintance we are naturally more guarded and cautious. Between close friends there often is no need for words because both people think and feel the same.

The highest and most beautiful consequence of friendship is the sharing of the good. A best friend always has the good of his companion in mind, whether that be a material or spiritual good. "To love is to cherish one thought, to live for the person loved, not to belong to oneself."[3] A good example of this mutual caring can be found in the first book of Samuel in the relationship between David and Jonathan, the son of King Saul of Israel. At one point King Saul was seeking the life of David out of jealousy, but Jonathan was David's best friend. He did all he could to speak well of David to his father and to protect him from harm. Once in a field outside of the city, Jonathan let David know that Saul wanted to kill him and that David had to flee. And they embraced one another with tears (see 1 Sam 20:41). Earlier, Jonathan had given David his own armor and sword, for, as the Bible states, "he loved him as his own soul" (1 Sam 18:3).

Because they share the good with one another, close friends warn each other of danger, either to body or soul, even with risk to themselves. If a friend has a bad habit or is making a fool of himself, his friend will let him know and try to deliver him from it. If one has discovered something good (like a worthwhile movie, website, book, or video), he will let his friend know of it. He will also try to connect him with people he will like and who can help him in his journey through life. In a word, a good friend is really like "another self."

In all of the above we can see the beauty and depth of human relationships and how they can form the basis for the greatest good of all: the communication of the truth and love that is Christ Himself. This is the ultimate and most powerful manifestation of friendship, but it needs a special grace from God in order to happen.

---

[3]   St. Josemaría Escrivá, *Furrow* (New York: Scepter, 1988), no. 797.

Finding Christ Together

Once again, we return to the life and work of Christ, who is the origin of all co-redemption. He is the Great Friend who became a human being to introduce us to His intimate family life: the Father, Himself, and the Holy Spirit.

Through the Church and her sacraments, He gives us sanctifying grace by which we share in His divine life and by which can know and love people and things like God Himself does. This power is given to us through the theological virtues of faith, hope, and charity, which are infused into our souls at Baptism.

But through the mystery of co-redemption we, too, can bring others to Christ and the marvelous supernatural life that He offers. All the things mentioned in the last section about human friendship can be the basis on which Christ Himself builds strong bonds between us as we try to be loyal friends to those we know. Let us recall that great theological principle enunciated by St. Thomas Aquinas many centuries ago: "Grace builds upon nature."[4] The greater our natural human friendship is with others, the more open it is to grace and supernatural life.

This principle has very practical consequences. If we know a person's family, for instance, it is easier to speak of God's love and knowledge of us. If we know a person's talents, we can more easily challenge him to help others and society in general. The more clearly we understand another's pain and suffering, the more readily we can lead him to the One who gives meaning to suffering, Christ on the Cross.

---

[4] See St. Thomas Aquinas, *Summa Theologiae* I-I, q. 1, a. 8, ad 2.

But we must not think that these things happen automatically. If we are to draw our friends closer to Christ, we must first pray for them. Prayer is necessary to obtain the grace our friend may need to understand and accept a difficult point of the Church's teaching, or simply to agree that she must change something in her life. Prayer is necessary to bring another out of sadness or despair so that she can see people and things with greater objectivity and hope. Prayer *with* a friend can show her a practical way to speak with Christ, the Great Friend who wants to elevate and save her.

Love that sacrifices is the greatest and most powerful way to bring someone closer to Christ because it most reflects how Christ saved us in His life and on the Cross. It is not simply a question of being kind or doing favors for others. To help others obviously has a human value, but sacrifice connected with Christ has the divine value of bringing grace into the world. This sacrificial love can be carried out in many ways. It can be shown in little things, such as assisting others in daily tasks. It can also be shown by offering up work, difficulties, or illness for a friend of ours; God in His infinite mercy of course will see our effort and will apply it to our friend in the way He sees fit. A friend with real sacrificial love gives himself completely, even to the point of danger or death, in order to save his friend from material or spiritual harm.

Sacrificial love is manifested in a marvelous way in the traditional corporal works of mercy: feeding the hungry, sheltering the homeless, clothing the naked, visiting the sick and imprisoned, and burying the dead. The spiritual works of mercy have even more value because they directly assist souls: instructing the ignorant, advising the doubtful, comforting the afflicted, correcting those in error, forgiving those who have offended us, bearing wrongs patiently, and praying for both the living and the dead.

The good friend does not force or coerce his friends to come closer to God. At most, he supplies the base or context upon which God's grace will move them. He always respects and values the freedom of his friends; he does not "nag" them into heaven but points out the way joyfully and accompanies them since he himself is also trying to improve and come closer to Christ.

St. Josemaría, using the Gospel parable of the wedding feast, would at times speak of a certain "holy coercion or forcefulness" as part of a Christian's apostolate. It is not a physical or psychological push, he would insist, but the cumulative effect of good doctrine, cheerfulness, and friendship of one person upon another. Its power really comes from God's grace working in the other person's soul through the relationship of a friend who prays and sacrifices for her and really loves her.

The best way to help a person is through the Holy Mass. By "putting a person on the paten" next to Christ we gain the greatest amount of grace for him or her. It is the closest we can come to Jesus's intimate action in a soul since by offering ourselves and our friend in the Eucharist with Christ, we bring the person to God Himself, who is the Source of all grace and mercy.

In the whole work of co-redemption, let us not forget the action of the angels. These powerful beings—pure spirits with intellect and free will—can be either our good friends or our enemies. The devil and his demons will tempt us against God's salvation, leading us to presumption or despair. They are the great enemies of repentance and conversion, and they can influence us strongly in our thoughts and imagination. For this reason, we need to remain close to the good angels, who can protect us and move us closer to God. Sound Catholic doctrine affirms that each of us has a guardian angel, or guiding spirit, who will keep us on the safe road and guard us from the evil one. We need to invoke our guardian angel frequently (it is not only a children's devotion) as we pray, work, travel, and particularly as we struggle against temptations. In the task of co-redemption, it is most helpful to pray to the guardian angel of our friend as well; our friend's angel is a powerful accomplice in bringing that person closer to Christ.

A loyal friend will not avoid correcting or warning his friend in time of need. Such is the difference between a mere acquaintance and a real friend. As we said earlier, the real friend cares enough to point out a serious or dangerous situation and has confidence that the other will listen to him. "If your brother sin against you, go and tell him his fault, between you and him alone" (Matt 18:15), Our Lord Himself tells us. He is continually correcting yet uplifting His disciples at the same time: with John and James who were too impulsive; with Thomas who was doubting; with Martha who was losing her peace and composure. Because He loves, He corrects.

Of course, we are only poor human beings who have our personal faults. We are not Jesus Christ, the perfect man. Therefore, when we must correct someone, we should consider first if we ourselves have the same fault and are struggling against it, though this does not nullify our duty to correct another for his good. We should pray for a person whom we need to correct so that he will understand us and respond well. Perhaps we could check with a good mutual friend about the best way to tell our friend what needs to be said. As we saw before in the section on the communion of saints, helping one another is part of the mystery of co-redemption.

So much of this mystery comes down to real service and humility. In the end, the true friend desires the good of his friend, and he is willing to inconvenience and sacrifice himself for the good of another. These actions are part of Christ's salvific plan for the human race, as we can see often in the writings of St. Paul. The Apostle indeed loves his fellow Christians and must correct and encourage them through his letters. He also suffers with them (see 2 Cor 2:1–4; Gal 4:19). His great dream is that all should have Christ dwelling within them and that they should be other Christs themselves. This should be our dream as well.

Never Alone

The authentic apostle, and therefore co-redeemer, never works alone. In her friendship with another, she will rely on the communion of saints and the network of graces that flow from this earth into eternity and back again. For this reason, she will pray to the angels and saints for her friends. She knows that she herself is limited and that she needs a lot of help from heaven to do good on earth. The closer she can unite herself to the Church and her saints, the more effective she will be. The more she prays and sacrifices, the more good she will do. As Christ Himself said, "I am the vine, you are the branches. He who abides in me, and I in him, he it is that bears much fruit" (John 15:5).

A true friend may lead his companion to great heights—perhaps to make a great conversion in his life, to have a new insight into the truth, to change his attitude toward another, to pray or repent more—but he realizes that he is never alone in his reaching out. Friendship entails companionship; the more a person helps another, the closer he comes to Christ. And in speaking to another about conversion or spiritual truth, he himself experiences a kind of conversion and comes to love and appreciate that truth more.

When there is co-redemptive friendship, both friends come close to God together. As a matter of fact, since friendship involves a certain equality and sharing of the good mutually, both help each other to get closer to God, though one of them may have more formation or clearer ideas about the faith and redemption. For instance, in helping a friend to overcome a sinful attachment or addiction, the true friend not only hears about it but in a way will also "suffer through it" with his friend, which is the etymology of the word "compassion." Being another Christ always entails compassion, or the ability to suffer with another.

Precisely by trying to assist his friend, the other person becomes more humble and enlightened. Such is the beauty and depth of Christian friendship, which forms part of the mystery of co-redemption.

CHAPTER 9

The Holy Mass: Center of Our Redemption on Earth

"Jesus ... having loved his own who were in the world, he loved them to the end." (John 13:1)

IT IS IN THIS WAY that the Evangelist introduces his account of the Last Supper. And his meaning is quite clear: Jesus Christ did not hold back in showing His affection for the Apostles—first by washing their feet, then by establishing the Holy Eucharist, then by giving them the new commandment that they should love one another as He had loved them.

The Holy Eucharist is the greatest outpouring of love and grace in human history because it re-produces and re-presents the great events of the Last Supper and Calvary. At the Last Supper, when He celebrated the Passover Meal with His disciples, Jesus established the New Passover and the New Covenant forever. At Moses's command, the Hebrews celebrated Passover before they escaped from Egypt, as we saw Chapter Three of this book. They sacrificed a young male lamb, put its blood on their doorposts, and consumed it with their families. As a result, the exterminating angel did not kill their first-born sons, as he did to the Egyptians, but he "passed over" the houses sealed with the blood of the lamb (see Exodus 12:13). In this way the Hebrews were allowed to leave the slavery of the land of Egypt and begin their journey to the Promised Land of Israel. It was the central event of Hebrew history and religion and was relived each year in a solemn way at the Passover Feast in Jerusalem.

It was precisely at the central meal of that Passover Feast that Christ instituted the Mass and the Eucharist. After saying the ceremonial prayers, especially the Hallel Psalms (113–118), He offered Himself to His Father in the form of unleavened bread and wine. He proclaimed the words of consecration that would be repeated by bishops and priests throughout the centuries: "This is my body, which is given up for you"; "This is my blood, which is shed for you." Then He distributed His Body and Blood to the disciples to eat. That complete offering of Himself was consummated on the very next day at His Crucifixion, when He gave up His body and blood to His Eternal Father for the remission of sins and the sanctification of the human race. On the third day after He was buried, He rose from the dead and appeared to His disciples. His obedience conquered sin on Good Friday; His new life conquered death on Easter Sunday.

This entire sequence of events—the Last Supper, Calvary, and the Resurrection—make up what we call the "Paschal Mystery of Christ." They are truly the center of human history and our redemption. They constitute the New Passover and the New Covenant of God's people; but this time it was not with the blood of an animal but with the blood of the Son of God Himself, who through His death and Resurrection brought life and hope once again to a fallen race.

The mystery of salvation did not end in AD 30, when these great events most likely occurred. The action of Christ is re-presented and renewed on altars throughout the centuries by priests who act in His name and with His power. "Do this in remembrance of me" (Luke 22:19), He told His Apostles, giving them the power to continue the offering and consecration of His Body and Blood and to confer that power on their successors throughout time. The Holy Mass, then, is the renewal of what happened on Calvary, though in an unbloody way. The priest and the victim are the same, Jesus Christ, who offers Himself as an infinite Person to another infinite Person, the Father, in the love of still another infinite Person, the Holy Spirit. All of the Eucharistic prayers at Holy Mass conclude with a doxology including all three divine Persons: "Through him, with him, in him, in the unity of the Holy Spirit, all power and glory and honor are yours, Almighty Father, forever and ever. Amen."

The Mass, therefore, is the closest we can come in this life to the mystery of redemption. Every time the priest celebrates it, every time the faithful unite themselves with it through their priestly souls, they are sharing in Christ's saving power and, in some way, redeeming the world. Their lives are transformed little by little into the life and sacrifice of the Savior. All that they do is somehow placed next to the Sacred Host and the Sacred Chalice and given a new supernatural meaning. For this reason the Second Vatican Council has called the Sacrifice of the Mass the "source and summit" of the Church's life.[1] It is the greatest sacrament of all, and in some way all the other sacraments lead to it and are consummated in it. It is the real pledge of eternal life,

---

[1] See Second Vatican Council, Constitution on the Sacred Liturgy *Sacrosanctum Concilium* (December 4, 1963), §10.

when we shall be united to Christ and His Father forever, and our bodies, risen from the dead, will be conformed to Christ's own risen body.

Of course, the Mass should always be attended with awareness and devotion. St. John Vianney, the patron saint of all diocesan priests, said the Holy Mass with the greatest fervor. He lived in nineteenth-century France and was the pastor of a small country church in the town of Ars, near Lyons. Often, his hands would tremble and tears would appear in his eyes as he held the Sacred Host because the reality of Christ's presence was so powerful in his mind and heart. People who attended his Masses actually came back to the Catholic Church after many years, and later made a sincere confession of their sins in order to receive Holy Communion once again. In our time, there are many stories of people who have been drawn to the Catholic Church simply by attending a Mass and witnessing its beauty and power. Perhaps you have a non-Catholic friend that you could invite to a Mass said by a holy and pious priest; you will probably need to explain a few of our Catholic beliefs, especially about the Real Presence of Christ in the Eucharist and His sacrifice, but you may be surprised at the results.

The Mass is the banquet of the people of God, and in a mysterious way it reflects the eternal banquet of heaven, where all the people of God are gathered together in perfect unity rejoicing and giving praise to Him forever. Since the entire Church is present at every Mass, even if there be only one priest celebrating, we should try to unite ourselves with those around us and the universal Church. For the early Christians, the Mass, or *agapéi*, was the very center of their personal and community lives. All of them, rich or poor, slave or free, of different races and tongues, were united in the Body of Christ. The whole people of God are called to unite themselves both to the redeeming Christ in the Eucharist and to their brothers and sisters in the faith around them. Though Jesus alone offers Himself to His Father at the Mass, all of us, His Mystical Body on earth and in heaven, are with Him and with each other.

The Greatest Source of Redemptive Power

Trying to grasp all of these things—and what I have written is just a glimpse of what really happens at every Mass—we can only give thanks and acknowledge the mystery of it all. Really the goal of our life, no matter what kind of work we do, where we live, or what age we are, is to unite ourselves with that tremendous action. It is the heart of our redemption. In the words of Pope St. John Paul II in his first encyclical, "The redemption of the world . . . is, at its deepest root, the fullness of justice in a human Heart—the Heart of the First-born Son—in order that it may become justice in the hearts of so many human beings."[2]

To put it colloquially, the Mass is truly "where the action is." The action is in a human soul, for Christ had a soul like ours, who truly obeyed the will of God to the ultimate degree, laying down His life and every drop of blood in order to buy us back from sin and darkness. Sin was a disobedience, a deliberate turning from the God of Love, but His Son turned Himself toward that God of love, bringing

---

[2] Pope St. John Paul II, Encyclical Letter *Redemptor Hominis* (March 4, 1979), §17.

all of us with Him. For this reason, John Paul II states that we were all reconciled in Him. Human nature, which had been twisted and deformed by sin, was rectified and made holy in Christ's own human nature as He sacrificed Himself completely for us.

From here it is not hard to see that our greatest privilege—and opportunity—is to unite everything that we do with the Sacrament of the Eucharist. If we are to be true co-redeemers and save this poor world from sin and confusion, we must unite ourselves with the Son of God in His sacrifice. That is the source of power and energy for our day. Perhaps you could compare the Mass to the hidden energy of an atom; when tapped it has immense power—not only to create an explosion but to give energy. Or you could compare it to the heat-filled, energy-filled center of a star, which gives light and warmth to a whole solar system, as our sun does for the earth. But even this analogy limps. For stars, despite all their heat and energy, are still limited and will one day fail. But the merits of Christ in the Holy Mass are infinite and will never fail.

Here is a prayer that you might find useful: *Lord, if I am to be a co-redeemer, I need to make the Mass the very center of my spiritual life. I need to keep going back to it, again and again, to receive the inspiration and strength that I need to become a saint and to redeem the world with you.* In this way we will reproduce the four principal actions that Christ accomplished at the Last Supper and on Calvary: He gave praise and adored God in the most perfect way; He asked for grace and forgiveness for all of us; He made atonement and reparation through His blood and suffering, thereby satisfying all punishment due to our sins; and finally, He gave thanks (the meaning of the word "Eucharist") because He knew that His offering, united with the Holy Spirit, was bringing grace and liberation to all men. Those are the same actions that we will carry out each day if we become true participants in His sacrifice. And with Him, we can "buy back" the world from darkness and sin.

Entering into the Mass

Our first step is to attend Holy Mass with devotion and attention. We have to make sure that our connection with Christ the Redeemer is deep and personal. For this reason, we should give the Mass our *full and active participation*.[3] This means to prepare for it well by praying beforehand and, of course, arriving on time for it—even a few minutes earlier, as many people do for an exciting movie or sports event. It means saying the prayers of the Mass with attention, for instance, the confession of our sins, the Nicene Creed, the Our Father, and many other responses. Let's try not to respond in a routine way in these prayers, even if we have done them many times before. They are prayers based on Scripture, and they contain the liturgical inspiration given by the Holy Spirit to the Church throughout the centuries. In the early Church, many Christians, both men and women, would recite the Apostles' Creed even as they were being tortured and put to death for their faith. For them it was a summary of their whole life and their motivating light and force.

If the Mass is truly the greatest event of our week or of

---

[3] See Second Vatican Council, *Sancrosanctum Concilium*, §11.

our day, we should dress well for it, with our hands clean and our hair combed. This is not meant to impress people or to be a mere external sign of respect; dressing well is truly a sign of love. It shows the Lord that we are willing to take the extra trouble to appear before Him in the most presentable and pleasing way that we can—without sloppiness or over-casualness. It is true that Christ is our greatest friend, and we must feel very close to Him, but He and His Father are also Almighty God, and we should act and dress accordingly because of their Presence with us at the Holy Mass.

At Masses in which hymns and parts of the liturgy are sung, we should also give our best. God will surely be pleased to hear His praises sung with love and good melody. Perhaps if we are off-key or do not have good voices, we could "sing in our hearts" by listening to the music of others and trying to pray with their words. God, who knows our talents and our limitations, will be pleased either way.

The way we genuflect upon entering the Church is also a sign of reverence and love. Whenever we cross the front of the tabernacle, either close by or at a distance, let's show our reverence by genuflecting slowly and with devotion. Christ is truly present there, and we want to connect all of our actions, our whole life, with Him.

But the best way to live the Mass well is to unite our intimate thoughts and desires with Christ as we go through the various parts of the Mass. First, we beg His forgiveness for our sins and confess our unworthiness to take part in this holy and infinite action. Then, in the Liturgy of the Word, we listen to the texts of the Holy Spirit, whether of the Old or the New Testament, and try to apply them to our lives. It could be a narrative or a prophecy, a miracle of

Christ or a parable—but each text surely has a meaning for us the Holy Spirit wants to communicate. If there's a homily, let's once again ask the Spirit to enlighten us so that we can understand what the preacher is trying to tell us and how his words can bring us closer to God and others.

The Profession of Faith is the opportunity to declare publicly, with our brothers and sisters in Christ, the main truths upon which we build our lives and our eternity. And the Prayer of the Faithful, if there is one, is a marvelous opportunity to present our petitions to God united with His people. Christ Himself said, "For where two or three are gathered in my name, there am I in the midst of them" (Matt 18:20). Therefore, even if the Consecration, the very center of the Mass, has not yet occurred, Christ is with us as we pray for the Church, world peace, the poor, and other intentions that we desire to present to the Giver of all gifts.

The Liturgy of the Eucharist is where the sacrifice actually begins. As the priest presents the bread and wine to God, which will be converted into Christ's Body and Blood, we can offer our entire day to God. "Blessed are you Lord God of all Creation. Through your goodness we have this bread to offer, which earth has given and human hands have made. It will become for us the bread of life."[4] We want to convert our entire day, with all of its actions and even sufferings, into the bread of life through the Sacrifice of the Mass. As co-redeemers, let's put the phone calls, the hours of work, the frustrations and annoyances that we must face, problems and temptations, our personal actions and witnessing for Christ—let's put all of them on the paten and in the chalice.

---

[4] From the Preparation of the Gifts in the *Novus Ordo* Mass.

In many Churches a family or group of individuals actually bring the hosts and wine to the priest; we can unite ourselves to them as we bring our actions to the altar as well, praying that God will be pleased with them.

At the end of the Preface, when we recite or sing "holy, holy, holy," we can ask our guardian angel to assist us. The angels surround the throne of God always, and they particularly gather around every Mass since the Son of God is present. As the Eucharistic Prayer begins, let's ask our guardian angel, along with the highest choirs of angels, to present our offering to God and help us to pay close attention to the words about to be said. Each Eucharistic prayer, though differing in length and liturgical history in the Church, has the same purpose. Each of them has the Consecration as its culmination.

As we pray silently the prayer of Consecration with the priest, let's present our petitions for the living and the dead: for a friend that we are hoping will return to the Church, for a relative who has just lost his job, for a woman who is having a difficult pregnancy, for peace in a certain part of the world, for a friend or relative who just died, or for those who have died some time ago. The souls in purgatory surround each altar and every Eucharist like so many hungry souls, holy poor *souls*, who desperately seek the healing graces that pour forth from the Sacred Body and Blood. Our petitions are in this way united to the Second Person of the Blessed Trinity, who is asking the Almighty Father for the same things with us, in the love and unity of the Holy Spirit.

We also commemorate the saints who accompany us at this moment, uniting around the Eucharist in heaven. We remember those great and generous men and women who gave their lives for Christ (the first Eucharist Prayer, also called the Roman Canon, has two lists of saints by name). We ask them to intercede and obtain graces for us so that we can be co-redeemers, as they were, and present our lives as a holocaust to God, as they did.

Let's not forget, particularly, that saints are very powerful on their feast days. As the universal Church honors them, they have great intercessory power with God. It is worthwhile asking the saint of the day, for instance, for specific help in overcoming some temptation, in getting a job completed, in speaking with someone about a difficult matter. Since saints have their "specialties," so to speak, it makes sense to ask them for help in those areas, not only on their feast days, but throughout the year. For instance, St. Nicholas (December 6) is an expert for obtaining financial help; St. Thérèse of Lisieux (October 1) for offering to God the little things of our day; St. Catherine of Siena (April 29) for the positive influencing of public opinion; St. Thomas More (June 22) for the laws and government of the country.

The Miracle of Consecration

At the culmination point of the Eucharistic Prayer is the great miracle of the consecration or transubstantiation. There, through God's power, the host will be converted into the Body of Christ, whole and entire, and remain present in a substantial way under the appearance of bread; there, the wine will be converted into His Blood while still retaining the appearance and taste of wine. It is the Real Presence of Christ, the same One who offered the Last Supper and died on Calvary. It is a reenactment of the sacrifice by which

Christ offered Himself to the Father for our salvation, the offering that He made at the Last Supper and on Calvary. The priest and victim are therefore the same at every Mass though offered in an unbloody way. Even if our minds cannot penetrate this ineffable mystery, we should try to appreciate the depth of what is going on.

For instance, when the priest holds up the Sacred Host, we can adore the Lord hidden under the appearance of bread. Perhaps we could pray the words of the theological virtues, infused into our souls at Baptism: "Jesus, I believe in you; Jesus, I hope in you; Jesus, I love you." Or we could say the words of St. Thomas, to which Pope St. Pius X attached an indulgence: "My Lord and my God" and at the elevation of the chalice: "My Jesus, have mercy." There are so many other invocations and prayers that we can use, available in good missals and spiritual books, or, we can say other personal aspirations our souls wish to express. The main point is never to remain passive or to get used to this sacred moment but to try to unite our entire life with the Holy One on the altar.

After the great doxology, "Through Him, with Him, and in Him . . . ," comes the Rite of Communion. We begin it by saying the words that Christ taught us: the Our Father. With Christ before us on the altar, we can address the Lord with confidence, the confidence of our divine sonship, as we ask for our daily bread and for His protection. It is the antecedent to our Holy Communion, when we shall be united to His Son in a most intimate and personal way.

St. Augustine once distinguished between receiving ordinary bread and the bread of life, the Eucharist. When we receive ordinary food, we convert it into our bodily substance, but when we receive the Eucharistic Christ, just the opposite happens. "You do not convert me into you, as you convert food into your flesh, but it is you who are changed into me."[5] With that thought, we can make our thanksgiving after receiving Communion. We have received the love of our life, the goal of our life, the energy of our life.

I cannot tell you what things that you should say to your Redeemer when you receive Him; they will be very personal and intimate things for sure. Remember that He is present in your body physically for at least ten to fifteen minutes after receiving Him. Perhaps you would simply like to pledge your service to Him as His disciple in this world. You can tell Him that you want to bring about His kingdom on this earth, an anticipation of His glorious kingdom at the end of time, which He will bring forth in His mysterious way. Or perhaps you will simply beg Him to heal you of pride, laziness, lack of faith, or other faults that are holding you back. If you don't understand something or are hesitant about what to do, it is the ideal moment to ask for light, like the blind man in the Gospel: "Master, let me receive my sight" (Mark 10:51).

Or maybe you would just like to rest in His presence with a special joy inside of you that no words can describe. You are with your greatest friend, the heart of your heart, to whom your whole life is going. You realize that when you receive Him in the Eucharist, which is His risen Body, you are also receiving all of paradise—the other Persons of the Blessed Trinity, the Blessed Mother and St. Joseph, and all the angels and saints.

Somehow all of this glorious mystery is inside of you for

---

[5]   St. Augustine, *Confessions*, bk. 7, §10.

just a few minutes. It is the source and culmination of your entire life, and it will give you the power to be a co-redeemer.

CHAPTER 10

The Slavery of Sin

AT THE END OF WORLD WAR II, Pope Pius XII wrote these thought-provoking words: "Perhaps the greatest sin in the world today is that men have begun to lose the sense of sin."[1] When we look at the history of the last century and see the devastating results of two world wars, justified in the name of national or ethnic pride, we can see that he was right. Add to that the immense destruction of human life produced by atheistic Communism, the killing of an entire generation of unborn children in the last part of the century, and the great number of divorces that have decimated families. In our own century we have witnessed the most ruthless and brutal attacks of terrorism, the aggressive and pervasive pornography industry, the active promotion of sexual immorality, and all kinds of political corruption. The picture is not pretty.

No wonder St. John Paul II and other spiritual leaders called these sins, and the whole human context that led to them and still promotes them, the *culture of death*. In addition to what man has done to man, the evil one has done great harm to the human race and continues to do so. One of his favorite strategies is to appear as a "liberator" who has our own best interests in mind. As you recall from the

---

[1] Pope Ven. Pius XII, "Radio Message of His Holiness Pius XII to Participants in the National Catechetical Congress of the United States in Boston" (Pontifical Palace in Castel Gandolfo, October 26, 1946).

first chapter of Genesis, the devil in the form of a serpent deceived Adam and Eve by promising them a godlike privilege—"knowing good and evil" (Gen 3:5)—if they would disobey God's command and eat the forbidden fruit. Such is the essence of all sin; it promises a pleasure or a liberation from God's law, but in the end, it destroys and enslaves the person disobeying it.

Though some of the images in the first three chapters of Genesis may be symbolic, the event described was certainly historical; a great spiritual disaster occurred at the beginning of the human race. Many religions besides Judaism have stories of how man lost his original happiness, though most of them blame the gods or the blind force of fate for it. The inspired Old Testament story, on the contrary, clearly puts the blame on Adam and Eve. Our first parents were given great gifts by God, including immortality and freedom from pain and suffering, along with the greatest gift of all, intimacy with God Himself. He was their friend, and they spoke with Him personally. Yet in a moment of pridefulness, tempted by the devil, they rejected God's goodness and protection. They wanted to determine their own law, not depend on Him.

Satan's trick worked, and it continues to work throughout the centuries. He portrays God or the Church as authoritarian or dictatorial and promises a self-determining liberation. Yet in the end, it is Satan who is the true dictator—and a merciless one: Adam and Eve, and all of their descendants, became subject to his power. There will now be pain, suffering, envy, and above all, death in the human race. Man's own nature was also weakened; he won't see clearly what is morally good nor desire to follow it. Strong emotions such as jealousy, anger, and lust will perturb his judgment.

That initial harmony between husband and wife was also broken; jealousy, discontent, and mutual accusation now begin to show themselves. Where there was an atmosphere of harmony and peace, there will be murderous violence, as we can see in chapter four of Genesis, when Cain kills his brother Abel because of jealousy. From there the human race will decline more and more, into ever-worse sins of violence and sexual perversity.

That sin, which the Catholic Church calls *original sin*, has been inherited by every human being that was ever conceived, with the exception of Jesus Christ and His Mother. Original sin did not corrupt human nature completely, but it greatly wounded it, making it prone to sins of pride, anger, and lust. The Hebrew Scriptures report that there were some good people in those primitive times at the beginning of the human race, such as Seth, Enoch, and Noah. But on the whole, the human race degenerated until God decided to destroy it and begin again. Such is the meaning of the famous Flood narrative (Gen 6–9).

Anyone who has lived a while can see the results of sin in their lives and those of others. You don't have to go back to the Bible to see it. From the child cheating at games in order to win, to the young man and woman having sex outside of marriage, to the businessman falsifying numbers to increase his profit, to the elderly woman continually gossiping about the faults of others. And as we mentioned above, all these individual sins are only compounded by the destruction of families and children that come from drugs, pornography, and alcoholism.

If we are going to understand the meaning of redemption, we should be aware of all that sin has done to people, including ourselves, painful and unpleasant though it be. In fact, it is by seeing the effects of evil that we can truly appreciate all the good that Christ brought into the world and all that Christ did to redeem us.

The Seven Deadly Sins

The tendencies wounding human nature from original sin are usually divided into seven capital sins (from the Latin *caput*, which means head) because they lead to many more. One of them is most likely our predominant fault, or a combination of them. Perhaps we've never thought of them, though they have probably troubled us all of our lives. It's good to put a name on them so that we can appreciate the need for redemption, first in our own lives and then in the lives of others.

The first is pride, the root of all sin, really. It's a disordered attachment to our own thoughts and feelings, and it has many tentacles: vanity, the seeking of praise or honor at all costs, the scorning of other people, the refusal to change or take good advice, and, worst of all, the determination to make our own way without God. It was the reason for the fall of Adam and Eve and also, according to ancient tradition, of the devil himself: out of pride he refused to obey God, the One who created him.

Anger is disordered frustration before trials and contradictions. It leads to sarcasm, insults, cursing, and all kinds of violence. Sometimes it can be hidden or suppressed, but in the end, it either lashes out irrationally or causes mental illnesses and anxieties. Like pride, it can also destroy the lives of individuals and families.

Greed or avarice is the disordered attachment to material things. It can lead to envy, covetousness, cheating in our work, even murder. The avaricious person doesn't really care about God or others; he simply wants money or other kinds of benefits. A person who is totally consumed by his work and forgets about his duties to others shows a kind of greed.

Gluttony is the disordered attachment to food and drink. Like the other sins, gluttony comes from a certain lack of wholeness within ourselves. Because we are not happy with ourselves, we can become restless and seek compensation in food or drink, especially alcohol, thinking that they will fulfill our deep need or make life more bearable. But in the end, they only make us lose our health, or we become addicted to them.

Lust, or the disordered desire for sexual pleasure, is similar. It's clear, from the first book of the Bible, that sex was meant for the union of man and woman within marriage—as "one flesh" in the words of Genesis 2:24. But since genital pleasure is strong (God made it that way, to encourage the procreation of children), it can lead to many other sins—masturbation, premarital sex, adultery, homosexual actions, contraception (having sex without being open to its natural consequences). It can also become a strong addiction, which destroys not only physical health but also the well-being of families and souls.

Laziness, or sloth, is the tendency to do the minimum in things, or, as Church Father St. Ephrem of Syria said, it is a certain sadness or despair in the face of doing good (either for God, ourselves, or others). It is a strange passiveness that insidiously convinces someone that he cannot change his life and that nothing is worthwhile. Laziness is the cause of many sins of omission, that is, the non-performance of our duties toward God and others.

Envy is discontent or anger because of another's good fortune. It is really the most demonic of sins: it is most likely that original sin came from the devil's envy. He was enraged that Adam and Eve had such happiness and favor with God, whom he had rejected. Envy can occur in our lives if someone gets a better grade than we or does better in a sports event; if someone has a more successful business or a more beautiful wife or girlfriend; even if someone seems to pray better than we do or seems to be holier than we are!

Personal sins can lead to a whole structure of evil within society. Where lust prevails, the sex industry can flourish, including bad movies and internet pornography—which is a multi-billion-dollar business. Greed can easily lead to corrupt government, either on the local or national level; it also leads to unethical business practices and fraud. There have been whole countries and societies that have been largely based on racial or ethnic pride, with disastrous consequences. Gangs and other dishonest groups thrive on people's vices and on their laziness or cowardice in confronting them and stopping them.

The Worm Inside

As we said above, all of this comes from a certain wounding of human nature, which gives it a tendency to evil. St. Augustine actually called sin a kind of nothingness because the sinner is only chasing a phantom of his own imagination or desire, which is not connected with his true good. To put the situation in a graphic way, you could say that sin is like an insidious worm inside of us that bores a hole into our soul so that we are not content with being good or doing good. St. Paul calls evil a mystery—how can we, who are basically good, go against what is good for us in order to do evil? "For I delight in the law of God, in my inmost self, but I see in my members another law at war with the law of my mind and making me captive to the law of sin which dwells in my members" (Rom 7:22–23).

One of the worst results of original sin was the darkening of the mind. Though the moral law does exist within us as a kind of truth or light given to us by God, we don't see it clearly at times, or we can deliberately turn away from it. As a result, it is easy to rationalize many actions that are intrinsically wrong—that is, actions that go against what is truly good for ourselves and others. The sins of other people in society, bad customs and habits, and peer pressure all add to this justification. Therefore, in corrupted societies you can have things that are sanctioned or even praised, such as cannibalism, abortion, suicide, euthanasia, and killing of the sick or elderly who are of no apparent use to others.

Even when we clearly see what is good or necessary, our wills can be disturbed by anger, fear, sadness, hatred, and other strong emotions. Before original sin, our first parents had their emotions under the control of their minds and wills; but after sin, their emotions began to run wild and disturb them. As their descendants, we have the same flaw within us. Though we are always free, it will be hard many times to choose what is morally right or oppose what is morally wrong. The tendency to pleasure is also strong, which can turn us away from virtue, as in the sins of gluttony or impurity.

The great St. Paul, who was the fearless herald of Christ's redemption to both Jews and Gentiles, felt this ceaseless battle going on within him—between good and evil. His words frankly express what all of us have felt at one time or another: "For I do not do the good I want, but the evil I do not want is what I do. . . . For I delight in the law of God, in my inmost self, but I see in my members another law at war with the law of my mind and making me captive to the law of sin which dwells in my members. Wretched man that I am! Who will deliver me from this body of death?" (Rom 7:19, 22–24).

Conquering the Evil One

Before Christ, people had very few defenses against the evil one or their own inner disorders. The devil's influence was particularly powerful before the coming of Christ: there were many possessed people (we can see this in the Gospels), and many others under demonic influence, such as those who worshipped false gods. Even the most advanced and intelligent pre-Christian peoples, like the Greeks, could not overcome their weaknesses and fell into intellectual soph-istry and sexual perversities like sodomy. Even their most exalted notions of God—such as the Prime Mover or the Supreme Form or Idea—did little to affect any real changes in human conduct.

It is true that the Greek philosophers proposed a life of virtue as the ultimate fulfillment of human beings—especially the adherents of Plato and Aristotle, and later on, the Stoics. But for the Stoics and many others there was no ultimate purpose or goodness behind the universe; men were taught to be good only for the sake of virtue itself or for their own sake—not for a good beyond themselves or for a Person who understood and loved them. The Stoic ideal was a rather sad and lonely life for a man who was trying to be virtuous.

Other ancient peoples tried to rid themselves of evil through sacrifices. They believed that they could be protected from hostile gods by sacrificing something valuable to them—like a new harvest of wheat, or a prized lamb or cow, or even a human being. In this way they hoped to propitiate their god so that he would forgive their transgressions or give them victory in war, good weather, or other benefits.

The Hebrew Scriptures also speak of sacrificing animals or crops. Though the Hebrews believed in the existence of only one God, far more exalted and different from the gods of other peoples, they, too, felt the need to offer Him things of value throughout the year in order to obtain favors from Him, to atone for their sins, or simply to commemorate the great events of their history. They offered special sacrifices on certain occasions—such as the birth of the first-born son in a family, the coming of the harvest, and above all the Passover, the commemoration of their liberation from the slavery of Egypt. By killing a lamb then eating it—or by burning an animal completely as a holocaust—they showed their complete dependence on God. As we saw before, the high priest on the feast of Yom Kippur would sacrifice two goats, one whose blood would be smeared upon the altar while the other was sent into the desert, loaded with the people's sins (see Lev 16).

These ceremonies in some way are an anticipation of the redemption that Christ would bring. For He, the Son of God Himself, is the most valuable being in the eyes of His Father—more valuable than any bull, lamb, or goat, or any offering done by mere human beings. He freely offered Himself in atonement for our sins. It was truly a holocaust of atonement and a new Passover, which put us at one (atone) with God again, something that no human effort could accomplish. To use an example from a childhood nursery rhyme, the human race and each of us before Christ were much like Humpty-Dumpty, who "had a great fall, and all the king's horses and all the king's men couldn't put Humpty together again." If you ever tried to pick up a broken egg on the floor and put it back together again, you'll get the idea.

Redemption is thus the restoration of justice, which was accomplished and fulfilled in the human heart of Christ; through His obedience to God, He radically canceled the disobedience of Adam and Eve and healed human nature of its sin in and through Himself. Because of His sacrifice and grace, we have balance restored to us once again—spiritual, mental, and emotional; we can identify and fight temptations more effectively, though we may still fall; we have a wholeness and completeness within us that makes us *right* with God and ourselves, which is really the meaning of justification, something very related to redemption; above all, we have the deep joyful conviction that we have been deeply loved, and this is a conviction far more powerful than any kind of sin or despair.

After original sin, God did point to this ultimate victory for mankind against evil. In the presence of the guilty couple, He told the serpent: "I will put enmity between you and the woman, and between your seed and her seed; he shall bruise your head, and you shall bruise his heel" (Gen 3:15). The human race therefore was not entirely lost by sin. Hope was given to us; for God announced the first Gospel, the *protoe-vangelium*, to Adam and Eve in symbolic terms.

As we know, subsequent history ultimately revealed the identity of this son of Eve who would conquer the evil one in the end. It was Jesus Christ who would convert the mystery of iniquity into the mystery of redemption. In the stirring words of St. Paul: "Where sin increased, grace abounded all the more, so that, as sin reigned in death, grace also might reign through righteousness to eternal life through Jesus Christ our Lord" (Rom 5:20–21).

CHAPTER 11

The Overwhelming Power of Charity

WE'VE ALL HEARD THE EXPRESSION, "Love makes the world go around." Maybe a better way to say this, looking at the Bible and the Church, is that "love created the world in the first place." When God created the universe, He freely chose to give being to creatures, sharing and making them a reflection of His own infinite goodness. He didn't gain anything by doing it, as you and I might gain money or praise for doing something worthwhile. No, God created us out of sheer goodness, and He does expect us to recognize and praise Him in His works, as much as we're able.

If there is truly one virtue or force that will redeem the world, it is charity. This virtue was given to all of us at Baptism, configuring us to Christ and giving us a share in God's own life. Charity has often been called the form and motivation of all the other virtues and good qualities that we might have. If we do things out of love for God and others, our actions have a certain beauty and power that they would not have otherwise. For instance, as we saw before, someone who does a simple task such as sweeping the floor does it much better when he does it out of love and thoughtfulness for all in the house. An elected official who truly loves his country and wants the good for its people will certainly do a better job—presuming that he is competent—than a person who is there simply for money or prestige. Charity adds thoughtfulness to whatever we do: it is the dimension of the "other" in our life that gives our own life quality.

Christ Himself gave a marvelous example of charity when He washed the feet of His disciples at the Last Supper. He who was the Rabbi and Master did this menial service for His followers and asked them to do the same for one another (see John 13:14). He then proceeded to show them the greatest service of all when He consecrated the bread and wine into His Body and Blood and gave Himself to them in the Eucharist. He summarized all that He did by giving them a revolutionary new commandment: that they should have love for one another (see John 13:34).

In the Early Church

This unselfish and heroic love for God and others was the driving force in the growth of the early Church. The understanding that Christians had for one another, and their spirit of mutual service, were astounding to the pagan world. Even as they were being thrown into prison or taken to the arena to be killed, they sang and consoled one another, trusting in God's power to take them to Himself after death and to give them a share in Christ's own victory. Their families were stronger and more cohesive than their non-Christian neighbors, and they were open to having children, though many Christian couples lived voluntary continence. As a matter of fact, Christians were known to go to the street corners where the pagans had left their unwanted children to be exposed and die; they would take these children into their homes and raise them to believe in Christ and His Church. They would teach them to pray, to honor the Roman government, to work hard, and to be chaste. Little by little, such actions and attitudes began to transform the entire ancient world—one person at a time, one family at a time.

The charity of the first followers of Christ went so far that they would take care of persons left in Rome to die during the frequent plagues. Not only did the Christians stay in Rome to take care of their own sick and dying, but they also took care of pagans who were sick and dying, left there by their relatives who ran from the city. When their non-Christian relatives returned, they could not believe the kindness of the Christians—whom they had ridiculed so much and persecuted. In a word, it was the love of Christ that was changing everything. Within a few centuries, because of Christian influence, that materialistic and violent empire radically changed. Divorce was not permitted, children were better treated and educated, and the gladiatorial games—in which two men or more fought to kill each other before bloodthirsty crowds—were eliminated, as was the gruesome and inhumane punishment of crucifixion.

Yes, *co-redemption* is the right word to explain the works of these first heroes of Christ, both men and women. And you can say that it is *your* work today.

Through prayer and, above all, charity, the hardest hearts can be converted. We find ourselves in a world largely built upon ambition, pleasure, and fear. The ambition for earthly success and comfort is all around us, as if this were the only life. To use a Gospel phrase, so many are looking for their treasures in this world, where only thieves break in and steal (see Matt 6:19). But the real treasure lies elsewhere.

A New Way of Thinking

The Christian virtue of charity brings a new logic to the world. In the words of Pope Benedict XVI in his third encyclical, the followers of Christ practice the "logic of gift."[1] To visit and feed people in a soup kitchen, to spend time with someone who is lonely or without friends, to give generously to a worthwhile project, to enlighten someone who is confused and depressed—all of these actions bring Christ's kingdom to the world little by little.

Love for God and others also elevates and purifies our way of looking at pleasure. When people hear the word pleasure, they often think of the pleasure of eating, drinking, or sex. Of course, none of these pleasures are bad in themselves, and they have a definite purpose for the good of the human race. But Christian love raises these pleasures to a higher level: that of giving praise to God. The Lord is worshipped when Christians eat or drink with moderation and when they reserve sexual pleasure to the union of man and woman in marriage, open to the mutual giving of love and life. In addition, Christians experience an even greater pleasure when they voluntarily sacrifice themselves for another; it is the same kind of pleasure, though often mixed with pain, that the great Catholic saints throughout the centuries experienced when they dedicated themselves to God and helped those in need—whether materially or spiritually.

So many people could do good if they overcame their fear of what others will say or think. "Oh, they'll think I'm

---

[1] Pope Benedict XVI, Encyclical Letter on Integral Human Development in Charity and Truth *Caritas in Veritate* (June 29, 2009), §§34, 36.

a fanatic if I go to Church every day." "Oh, they'll think I'm old-fashioned if I don't tell dirty jokes." "Oh, they'll think I'm ignorant if I say that I believe in certain ideas." And perhaps the worst of all: "Oh, they'll think I'm being judgmental if I say that some action is morally wrong and should never be done." Peer pressure can be very strong. It affects children at school, couples in their homes, businessmen and politicians in their work. It creates a kind of fear of being different, and people end up like paralytics when it comes to doing good.

The Gospel gives us the answer: "Perfect love casts out fear" (1 John 4:18). If we speak cleanly and refuse to tell impure stories, it is because we love God and others. If we go to Church frequently, it is love that motivates us to do so and encourage others to do the same. If we believe in ethical principles involving right and wrong, it is because we love what is good and follow the moral law—without which there is no real happiness for anyone. In this way, charity is indeed an overwhelming force that can transform lives in our century, as it did centuries ago in early Christian times.

St. Paul summarized the greatness of charity (or "love," in many Scripture translations) very forcefully in his famous letter to the Corinthians: "If I speak in the tongues of man and of angels, but have not love, I am a noisy gong or a clanging cymbal. And if I have prophetic powers, and understand all mysteries and all knowledge, and if I have all faith, so as to remove mountains, but have not love, I am nothing. If I give away all I have, and if I deliver my body to be burned, but have not love, I gain nothing" (1 Cor 13:1–3). In other words, it is possible to be a very impressive individual with many talents and gifts, but ultimately to be a failure if we do not know how to love. Great wisdom, great faith, heroic sacrifices, even great generosity to the poor would mean nothing if there was no love for God and for others behind them.

St. Paul's words are rather frightening. They make us examine our intentions frequently—in our work, with our families, even in the way we live our religion. For it is quite possible for selfishness and egotism to take over in all these areas of our life, including religious practices, and we could end up as hypocrites. But the beautiful thing about charity is that it is simple and sincere; it does not do good for show or effect. It is truly God's love transforming the world and us. It is God's love that redeems and co-redeems, not our own generosity or good will.

Love's Expansion to Others

But how can we obtain charity? One clear answer is that we cannot obtain it with our own efforts or willpower. It is a supernatural virtue or gift that we received at Baptism, and it grows with each sacrament we receive. It is something that we must beg God to increase in us, for it can easily be reduced to mere human generosity or good will—which often has mixed motives behind them, like the story of the man who began an orphanage simply to get his name in the newspaper, or someone who donated to a good cause so that he could make friends with rich people. Charity is best done in quiet so that only God sees the love behind it. As Jesus said, "Thus, when you give alms, sound no trumpet before you, as the hypocrites do in the synagogues and in the streets, that they may be praised by men. . . . But when you give alms, do not let your left hand know what your right hand is doing, so that your alms may be in secret" (Matt 6:2–3).

Charity has a number of "little brothers," so to speak, that are also important. One is kindness and another is good humor. We should learn to say things in a positive way, without putting people down. Irritating or sarcastic remarks in the end will backfire on us, though we may get a momentary reaction by yelling or blurting something out. There is nothing like a genuine smile—not an ironic one—to put people at ease and help them to listen to us, and we to them. If every person sincerely beseeched the Holy Spirit to move them to say and do everything for love of God and others, we would soon have a different world, and Christ's kingdom would spread very quickly on earth.

Another whole area for practicing charity is the use of our tongue. One of the greatest causes of dissension in human society is gossip and backbiting. It undermines trust for one another in society; it can destroy the atmosphere of a school or business; it can poison a home. Real charity teaches that we should not reveal the faults of others unless there is a serious reason. If a person is a drug peddler making advances, you will have to warn others about him or her. If a college professor has anti-Christian bias and continually attacks the Church, you should be on guard and warn your friends also. This is not gossip but authentic charity that has the good of others in mind. Parents have the right and duty to speak to each other about their children, including their faults, in order to help them; employers have the same right to speak of their employees' performance in order to help the business; friends have the right to speak to their friends about those who could harm them.

With real charity, you can be a true instrument of redemption wherever you are. The best thing is to say what is good and needed at the right time, without falling into loquacity or frivolous conversation. Often you will just have to be silent rather than contribute to a bad conversation. "If you cannot praise, say nothing," the old saying goes. There is great wisdom behind that. Oftentimes we must simply be humble and realize that we do not have all the facts in a case and are in no position to judge another person's motivations.

At the same time, Christian charity is not soft like cotton candy, nor is it to be "nice" all the time. To be nice does not always mean to be *good*. It could come from an obsessive desire for being popular or liked by others at all costs. Certainly, it is not charity to let someone fall into sin or to hurt his or her physical or spiritual health. Often people will not speak up to help others because they don't want to be judgmental, which is a false excuse. Real charity for others at times means correcting them. It is not being mean or old-fashioned to correct someone; the Redeemer Himself says that fraternal correction is good and necessary. "If your brother sins against you, go and tell him his fault, between you and him alone" (Matt 18:15). We can do immense good for a person who doesn't realize his fault or who sees it only in a vague or confused way. In the meantime, he could be hurting himself or even making enemies, like the story of the man in the office who was always late for his appointments. He had a nice enough personality, but many people would complain behind his back because of his tardiness. No one told him that he had to improve in this area, and in the end, he was fired from his job without ever being told why. It is true that some people don't want to be corrected or may become resentful if you try to tell them something that they need to improve. In which case, you can always keep praying for them then try to bring up the problem in another way at the right time.

There is no real advancement in our spiritual life unless we practice charity, which is the greatest virtue of all. "Most Sacred Heart of Jesus, expand my heart!" If we are to do any good on this earth, somehow our hearts and desires need to be modeled on Christ. We need to look at people and the world through a new set of eyes. The Gospel states that when Jesus saw the crowds, He had compassion on them (see Mark 8:2). Often when we look at crowds, we can become annoyed or bothered because they are in our way, or we may be tempted to scorn people who look strange or ridiculous to us. Perhaps they are the ones who need our prayers the most.

In other words, we need to be *merciful* to others. Mercy is that part of charity that sees another person's need and responds to it. It is opposed to a selfish view of life and converts us into true co-redeemers. We can truly say that God made the long journey from eternity into time because He loved us and had mercy on us. Our Lord died on the Cross and rose again because of us—to bring us forgiveness and eternal life. As Pope Francis wrote in the Bull of Indiction for the Holy Year of 2015, "Jesus Christ is the face of the Father's mercy ... Mercy [is] the bridge that connects God and man, opening our hearts to the hope of being loved forever despite our sinfulness."[2]

Ultimately it is *deeds* that count. We can have a lot of

---

[2] Pope Francis, Bull of Indiction of the Extraordinary Jubilee of Mercy *Misericordiae Vultus* (April, 2015), §§1–2.

good humanitarian feelings toward others, but unless we can translate those feelings into actions, they remain only feelings. If charity is like a fire, it must be fed with more and more twigs and logs. To visit a sick person, to help a friend who is mistaken or misguided, to cheer up someone who is sad or lonely, to give money to a family facing poverty—these are deeds that truly transform the world for Christ. And in doing them, we ourselves are transformed: this is one of the central truths of co-redemption.

CHAPTER 12

Making Atonement:
Redemptive Sacrifice

"And as they led him away, they seized one Simon
of Cyrene, who was coming in from the country,
and laid on him the cross, to carry it behind Jesus."
(Luke 23:26)

WE DON'T KNOW TOO MUCH ABOUT SIMON, the man who
was forced to carry Jesus's Cross, except that his two sons
became Christians and were well known afterwards. Simon
must have been a good Jew fulfilling his duty at the Passover Feast, and had the misfortune—or the fortune—to be
among the crowd looking at Jesus as He carried the Cross
through the streets to Calvary. Perhaps he had heard something of the wonder-worker and preacher from Galilee, but
he certainly was not expecting to end up carrying His Cross.
And yet, by doing so, he contributed to our redemption.

At times God will send us unexpected crosses—
extra work, a rude remark, a sickness, a sleepless night.
With a co-redemptive mentality, we will see these things
as opportunities to work with Christ in redeeming the
world and indeed in sanctifying all of human experience. For suffering is a great equalizer among men. Not
everyone can reach God through intellectual effort or
a life of continuous prayer or virtue. But all of us can

suffer, either physically, mentally, or spiritually. And it is that suffering that can lead us to God in a way that other experiences cannot.[1]

To be crucified in ancient times was the most humiliating way to die. Apart from the intense pain of the nails driven into his hands and feet, the victim suffered a slow and inexorable asphyxiation. His body collapsed and his lungs needed to breathe, but every time he wanted to lift himself, he experienced the unbearable pain of the nails. Roman citizens could not be crucified; it was considered too cruel. Yet such was the cost of our salvation. It was through His blood and pain that the Son of God bought us back from the power of the devil and of sin. Through that blood and pain, He reconciled the human race with God and brought forgiveness into the world. If we truly wish to be other Christs and to redeem others with Him, we will desire to unite ourselves in some way with the Savior's sufferings.

St. Paul, who experienced suffering for Christ most intensely in his own life, even speaks of the cross as a kind of glory: "But far be it from to me to glory except in the cross of our Lord Jesus Christ, by which the world has been crucified to me, and I to the world" (Gal 6:14). That must have been a shocking statement to make back in those times. It is as if someone were to say today: "It's necessary for us to glory in lethal injection." But the mystery of Christianity is precisely that: it is through pain and rejection that true liberation, including joy, will come—as long as that pain and rejection have been offered generously to God.

[1] See Servais Pinckaers, *The Pursuit of Happiness—God's Way: Living the Beatitudes* (New York: Alba House, 1998), 80–90.

We must always bear in mind that the human race was not saved through human accomplishments or progress. It was not a thriving economy that brought lasting hope to human beings; it was not a strong military force that conquered the evil one and his demons; it was not any kind of technical or scientific advance that produced true liberation. Redemption was accomplished by one man shedding His blood, with the most intense kind of pain, surrounded by mockery, on a hill just outside of Jerusalem two thousand years ago. And somehow, if we are going to be co-redeemers, we must never forget it.

Mortem Facere: *The Good Death to Self*

"If any man would come after me, let him deny himself and take up his cross and follow me" (Matt 16:24). In an age that prizes luxury and convenience, this saying of Christ is hard to accept. In an age when people flee from any kind of pain or extra effort, Christ's message is shocking and jolting. We, too, can be affected by the same kind of thinking but must learn to resist it bravely. As a matter of fact, the more we carry within us the suffering of Christ, the more powerful we will be. It gives us both supernatural endurance and courage.

St. Paul put this truth very dramatically in writing to the Corinthians, many of whom had come from soft, immoral lifestyles before their conversion. He reminds them not only of their fragility but also of their real strength in Christ: "We have this treasure in earthen vessels, to show that the transcendent power belongs to God and not to us. . . . For while we live we are always being given up to death for Jesus' sake, so that the life of Jesus may be manifested in our mortal flesh" (2 Cor 4:7, 11).

In many ways, we, too, must carry our cross each day and, in a certain way, be given up to death and pain. The college student who suffers because her roommate refuses to listen when she tries to explain to her that premarital sex is wrong. The dad who must endure a painful or unrewarding job to support his family. The mother who must keep up her strength and good humor each day for the sake of her children. The young professional man who loses friends because he refuses to go to parties where people get drunk. All of these are examples of co-redemption. These men and women are carrying within them the dying and rejection of Christ— but it is a death that will lead to life if they persevere.

Life has many sufferings, but moral suffering is often the hardest of all. It is easier to suffer through a bad headache or flu than to hear a person attack what is sacred and important to you without the ability to do anything about it. You just have to offer it to God and endure it. For this reason, Mary the mother of Jesus is the greatest co-redeemer. She could do nothing to stop the Crucifixion of her Son. She just had to stand there and endure it. And yet her offering and sacrifice with her Son were very powerful. Ours can be the same if we learn how to unite our sufferings—whether physical or moral—with the Virgin Mother and her Son. She is truly the *Co-Redemptrix* par excellence, as we will see in the last chapter of this book.

Lord, may I not be soft or comfort-seeking! If we are to do some good in the world, we need to die to ourselves, to get rid of the old person inside. This process is called mortification and has great power in our lives. The word mortification actually comes from two Latin words: *mortem* and *facere*, which together mean "to produce death." It means much more than simply being embarrassed, which is its most frequent use in English today. To practice mortification for self-sacrifice and love of God is one of the greatest things we can do on earth. If we know how to die for Christ and for others, we shall truly live and give life to the world.

Purification and Atonement

The first purpose of mortification is purification. We cannot be co-redeemers if we do not experience redemption in ourselves.

For instance, if I note that I tend to be proud and conceited in my reactions, I'll have to struggle against them, perhaps with the help of a good friend or spiritual advisor. Maybe I need to listen more to others or do favors for them. When I take time to pray and ask God's help for something, I also mortify pride inside of me—since the proud person thinks he can do everything himself and doesn't need to pray. If I realize that I'm lazy, I must learn to get up at a fixed time each morning (which often means going to bed at a reasonable hour); I should also do my work promptly, especially that part of my work that I find boring or tend to delay. If I'm too pleasure seeking, I can learn to fast on certain days of the week (for instance, Wednesdays and Fridays, which used to be called the Ember Days in the early Church), or give up snacks or sweets. If I tend to over-drink, then I should abstain from alcohol or limit myself to one or two glasses only. If I tend to become sad or melancholic about things or people, I should say more prayers and aspirations of hope, such as: "You, O

Lord, are my hope and salvation"; "All things for the good for those who love God"; "Mary, cause of our joy, pray for me."

In all of the above practices, it particularly helps if we smile, even force a smile if we need to, before hard situations and personal frustrations. The sacrifice of being patient with people who annoy us is also one of the best means to obtain holiness of life.

A good part of our struggle is to begin again. Perhaps we could call this "spiritual grit," as a good priest friend of mine once termed it. It has to do a lot with spiritual athletics, the ability to keep working for the Gospel of Christ that St. Paul speaks about in his letter to the Corinthians (1 Cor 9:24–27). If we have set goals for ourselves and we fail, we must not quit or give into discouragement. We know that our goal is Christ and that He will always pick us up from our falls, though they be very frequent. Of course, we are sorry for our sins and failings, but with the help of frequent Confession and with trusting acts of hope in God's grace, we return promptly to our struggle. As St. Mother Teresa, who herself had to face long periods of doubt and sorrow in her life, once said: "I do not pray for success; I ask for faithfulness."

It is hard to think this way always, but, in fact, God does give us successes now and again to encourage us. We just need to open our eyes and see them. The main point is to keep doing His will again and again—and not to give up despite apparent lack of success in our efforts. Such an attitude will conquer the world in the end. "Not everyone who says to me, 'Lord, Lord' shall enter the kingdom of heaven, but he who does the will of my Father who is in heaven" (Matt 7:21).

Voluntary sacrifice has another redemptive effect. It makes *atonement* or *reparation* for sin; literally, it puts us *at one* with God again. As we mentioned before, atonement is what Christ did on the Cross by shedding His blood and by conforming His will perfectly to God's will, thereby reversing what sin did to the human will. We, too, can make atonement if we unite our sufferings and mortification with Christ. When we sacrifice something to God, we are putting His honor and will above our own, as when we sacrifice to make time for prayer or to help a person in need. These generous actions make us truly one with God since they get rid of the obstacle between us and Him, namely, our own selfishness.

Again, it is St. Paul who enunciates one of the great principles of co-redemption when he writes to the Colossians: "Now I rejoice in my sufferings for your sake, and in my flesh I complete what is lacking in Christ's afflictions for the sake of his body, that is, the Church" (Col 1:24). We must understand this properly, of course, as we explained in the Introduction. Since Christ was the Son of God and His sacrifice was infinite and perfect, there can be nothing lacking in it. It redeemed all people of all times. But through His goodness, Christ enables *us* to connect our sufferings with His so that, in a personal way and throughout different times and circumstances, we, too, can bring redemptive grace to others.

Atonement or reparation is not simply a redemptive term. Often in society we hear of debtors having to make reparation for offenses, businesses needing to make reparation to private homes for property damage, restitution in lawsuits, etc. It is part of the virtue of justice to make reparation for damage done either to property or to a person's good name.

Children are often told to "make up" for their squabbles or offenses and return what they took from another. On a much larger scale, Christ made up for the sins of the world to the One who was primarily offended—Almighty God—and we, too, can do our part to make atonement in union with Him.

Concerning our own sins, of course we should confess them and do the penance as soon as possible. But in addition to that, it's very helpful to make some kind of voluntary atonement for them, even though the priest does not ask us to do so: if we've been rude, we should apologize; if we've gossiped about someone, we should restore his good name; if we've been lazy, we should do our duties better the next day. In donating to the poor for the love of Christ, we can make up for past sins of selfishness. By taking a cold shower or sleeping on the floor, we can atone for past sins of impurity or intemperance.

In the same way our sacrifices, when done in union with the Cross of Christ, can make up for the sins of others, even though they be very grave. Sins against human life such as murder and terrorist acts; sins against the family, including immoral legislation; sins of the flesh such as drunkenness and sexual promiscuity can all be atoned, with the help of God's grace, by our own efforts to be temperate and chaste in thought and action. By offering our own sufferings, we *enter the wounds of Jesus crucified* (to use a graphic expression of St. Josemaría Escrivá)—and make reparation to God for these grave sins. By obeying the Church loyally, we can also make up for the pride and rebellion of many people against the Church over the last fifty years.

How all of this can happen is a mystery. It requires faith, for it is not often (perhaps ever) that we will actually see the results of our sacrifices. The real effect is in the Sacred Heart of Christ in heaven, in union with the Father and the Holy Spirit. Only they know the true result of our voluntary sacrifices and pain. As co-redeemers, we can go through heart-wrenching pain and disappointment and literally receive no reward on earth except the knowledge that we tried. For instance, the college student who tries to convince her friend to be chaste with her boyfriend, as mentioned before, may not only lose her friend but may also be shunned by her classmates. The young fellow who challenges his teacher for his biased presentation of Christianity may fail the subject or be considered a "religious fanatic" by his classmates. The young professional who refuses to enter a fraudulent business deal may be fired or even blacklisted from other jobs.

And there are many other kinds of cases that are real tragedies, such as that of a young mother with three children who contracts malignant cancer or who is killed in a car accident. Why does God permit these things? We can only trust in His goodness and realize that redemption will often mean suffering that makes us very much like Jesus on the Cross when He cries out in agony: "My God, my God, why have you forsaken me?" (Matt 27:46). In His human mind and feelings, He was experiencing only terrible darkness and bitterness, yet at that precise moment, He was redeeming the world.

The Grain of Wheat

Voluntary sacrifice has another marvelous effect, just as powerful as atonement. Suffering with Christ brings grace and hope to the world. Let's not forget the *complete* mystery of

151

Christ, which includes His death as well as His Resurrection. Calvary is not the end of the story: Easter Sunday is the culmination of Christ's life. There is an ultimate victory behind the pain and suffering. Christ Himself put it in a very practical way, which everyone can understand: "Truly, truly, I say to you, unless a grain of wheat falls into the earth and dies, it remains alone; but if it dies, it bears much fruit" (John 12:24).

Through our voluntary sacrifices, as co-redeemers, we really become that grain of wheat which brings life and hope to the world. I recall a story about a ten-year-old boy who was diagnosed with bone cancer shortly after the Second World War. In those days they did not have the extraordinary treatments we have today for that disease. The parish priest of the boy's family would visit him often, bring him Holy Communion, and tell him jokes and funny stories. They helped for a while; the little fellow tried to smile, but he could not hide his pain, which was with him constantly. One day the priest had an inspiration. "Would you like to do some good with your pain?" he asked the boy. Right away the small cancer victim answered, "Sure I would," with a kind of eagerness in his voice, as if it were a game. "Well you know," said the priest, "there are lots of people suffering right now in Japan after the war, and there are not very many Christians there. Why don't you offer your pain for their conversion to the Catholic Church?" The little lad said that he would with the same kind of eagerness in his voice. The next day, the priest came to visit the boy and asked him how his night had been. "Oh, it's been terrible, Father. I couldn't sleep at all. My bones feel like they're on fire, and I have this awful thirst in my mouth—but I bet a thousand people converted in Japan." The priest's eyes began to water with tears when he heard that, though he tried to hide them from the child. Only God knew if anyone converted in Japan, but that didn't really matter. What really mattered was the boy's faith and generosity; and the priest knew that he had just witnessed something very beautiful.

St. Josemaría describes the challenge and mystery of co-redemption in his reflection on the fourteenth station of the Cross: "We must bring into our life, to make them our own, the life and death of Christ. We must die through mortification and penance, so that Christ may live in us through love. And then follow in the footsteps of Christ, with a zeal to co-redeem all mankind."[2]

Such is the hidden power of sacrifice and suffering if you really believe in Christ's redemptive power and His desire to share it with us. There are so many things for which we can confidently offer our own sufferings, big or small. When they are "plugged in to" the crucifix, they bring grace to the world. Even the toughest, most insoluble situations can be overcome by prayer and sacrifice. At times people's attitudes and hearts seem to be made of stone. But if you really believe in the sacrificial power of suffering united to Calvary, you can bring real conversions to the world and transform it. Remember Pope Benedict XVI's confident and challenging words at World Youth Day in Madrid: "Dear friends, may no adversity paralyze you. Be afraid neither of the world, nor of the future, nor of your weakness. The Lord has allowed you to live in this moment of history so that, by your faith, his name will continue to resound throughout the world."[3]

---

[2] Escrivá, *The Way of the Cross*, 120.
[3] Pope Benedict XVI, "Homily of His Holiness Benedict XVI" (World Youth Day, Prayer Vigil with Young People, Cuatro Vientos Air Base, Madrid, Spain, August 20, 2011).

CHAPTER 13

Sanctifying Illness
and Suffering

ONE OF THE MOST powerful means of co-redemption is the offering of suffering and illness for others. In some way, it is the closest to what Christ did for us on the Cross. Though He was not ill, He freely accepted God's plan for Himself and others by taking all human illness upon Himself and reversing the selfishness of the human will by His obedience to His Father. By putting Himself completely in the hands of God, He demonstrated His complete trust—as people who are ill or suffering must also do many times. And as a result of that generous gift of self, grace and redemption come into the world.

Human suffering and illness have a twofold source. The first is simply the weakness of the human race due to original sin. God's creative plan at first was to give our first parents freedom from the pain of sickness and death, but sin closed this door for us. Illness, then, such as heart disease, cancer, and infection, come from our fallen state, whether it be caused by genetics or factors outside of ourselves. The second cause of illness or suffering is often our own neglect or selfishness, such as the abuse of alcohol or drugs, diseases transmitted from sexual immorality, or simply our own imprudent behavior.

But no matter what the cause, all illness is an opportunity to win grace for ourselves and others if we accept it and offer it generously. Illness and suffering, whether physical, mental, or spiritual, can purify us from pride and self-sufficiency.

Since we must often be helped by other people—nurses, friends, family members—we can grow in gratitude as well. The various kinds of treatment given to us (whether medicines, tests, or therapy) give us the chance to be more patient and humble; hopefully, by being so, we can win grace for others as well as for ourselves. The story of the little boy with cancer in the previous chapter is significant: without knowing the meaning of the word, and thinking that his prayer was almost like a game, the child was being a co-redeemer. We must surely believe that God does great good with our sufferings though often they cannot be calculated in statistical terms. So it is with most human suffering on earth.

I recall the story of one of the first female members of Opus Dei, María Ignacia Escobar, who offered her sufferings from tuberculosis for the intentions of St. Josemaría, the founder of Opus Dei. She was introduced to Opus Dei by a young hospital chaplain, Fr. Jose María Somoano, who was taking care of her, and was greatly inspired by the message and spirit of his young friend Fr. Josemaría. Fr. Somoano asked her to offer her sufferings so that Opus Dei would have foundations of granite, to be laid by souls with a great love for Jesus Christ. She responded generously and wholeheartedly. Later on, Fr. Somoano himself would give his life for the Church and for the patients at the hospital where he was serving.[1]

---

[1] See John Coverdale, *Uncommon Faith* (New York: Scepter Publishers, 2002), 107–12.

But apart from illness there are many other sufferings in life. There is the suffering that comes from frequent misunderstandings and arguments in families. The constant willingness to forgive and try again not only brings relief but can also be a positive co-redemptive force. At times, even though difficult, people will need to have a sincere heart-to-heart conversation about certain issues that have to be faced together. This, too, can bring grace and understanding to certain situations and boost the morale of the entire family.

Suffering from financial anxiety can lead to greater trust in God. In a materialistic society, where so many put their trust in money or things, financial stress can be a great corrective and help people to focus on what really matters: their connection with God and His providence. Our Lord put this very clearly at the Sermon on the Mount: "Therefore do not be anxious, saying, 'What shall we eat?' or 'What shall we drink?' or 'What shall we wear?' For the Gentiles seek all these things; and your heavenly Father knows that you need them all. But seek first his kingdom and his righteousness, and all these things shall be yours as well" (Matt 6:31–33).

Perhaps the greatest human sufferings come from loneliness or despair—or the mental illnesses that are related to them. If we think that we have no friends, if we find no love from others, we should first consider if these thoughts are our own illusions or inventions. At times we are not objective about things, and we may not even notice or be open to others' love for us. But if the loneliness or despair continues, we can only turn to our greatest friend, Jesus Christ the Redeemer. This in itself is a redemptive act for ourselves since it is the way of getting out of our loneliness and anxiety by turning to another. And that other is Christ

Himself, who comforts and strengthens us in the power of His Sacred Heart.

But what if God does not seem to listen to us? Again, this can be deceptive because God always listens and responds; it is we who do not hear Him or trust Him.

But there could be authentic dark night moments in our life at times, which would involve the greatest of sufferings, similar to what Christ Himself must have experienced on the Cross. "My God, my God, why have you abandoned me?" (Matt 27:46), He cried out. Our Lord was obviously making His own the beginning words of Psalm 22, the prayer of a man suffering greatly from pain and persecution and who feels totally deserted by God. The Holy Spirit and the Fathers of the Church grant us a deeper exegesis: by these words Christ reveals that in Himself, in His human mind and heart, He was experiencing a great distancing between Himself and His Father at that moment, when He was taking upon Himself the sins of all mankind; when in the words of St. Paul, God "made him to be sin" in order to save us all (2 Cor 5:21). In other words, He was making Himself guilty of all the murders, all the adulteries, all the betrayals of men and women throughout the ages . . . and by doing this He was excluding Himself from the loving gaze of His Father, at least in His human consciousness. And yet, in this very act, He was healing us from within and redeeming us on the Cross.

Of course, none of our sufferings on earth can compare to what Christ endured. Yet in our own lives we can experience something similar. Perhaps we can feel overwhelmed by the enormity of sins in the world, our own included, and there seems to be no remedy for them. Or we can experience what Pope Benedict XVI called the "silence of God," when He apparently does not respond to us; that is, it seems to us that God is far away or doesn't care about what we are going through, or that we have prayed to Him again and again, but He has not answered our prayers.[2] This is when we can realize that, precisely at these moments, He is closest to us and will not abandon us. Or, as Pope Benedict XVI affirms, He is speaking to us through the mystery of His silence.[3] If we are to be like Christ, we must learn to offer these agonizing moments for those who need more help than we do or those with no faith at all.

This is co-redemption indeed, closely connected to what Christ accomplished on Calvary. One point to recall is that we must really experience *Christ's* Cross in order to co-redeem, not one of our own making. Sometimes people will complain of their many "crosses," but these "crosses" are simply the result of their own softness or overheated imaginations. They may actually be wasting time, neglecting work or prayer, forgetting about the needs of others, or be only focused on their own gratification. At times they also could be the victims of obsessions or mental illness, which may not be their fault, but which can also be given to God and accepted humbly. The main point is that it is only the Cross of Christ that sanctifies and redeems us; the more we can unite ourselves with *that* Cross, the more co-redemptive our words and actions will become.

---

[2] Pope Benedict XVI, Post Synodal Exhortation on the Word of God in the Life and Mission of the Church *Verbum Domini* (September 30, 2010), §21.

[3] Pope Benedict XVI, *Verbum Domini*, §21.

The Grace of Final Perseverance

The final days and moments of a person on earth will always have a particular intensity. If the person has adequate use of his mind or faculties and realizes that his time is short, certainly all kinds of thoughts can come to his mind: memories of his family and relatives, past experiences of his life, remorse for sin, hopeful thoughts about heaven, or despairing thoughts about his situation and the next life. Even if he is on artificial life support, who can say what his mind and heart are experiencing as he nears the end of his life? In terms of redemption, these final moments are the most important ones because they immediately precede his individual judgment before God.

God continues to love and to "knock at a soul's door" down to the last instant in order to bring a person to repentance and to the right condition of mind and heart to appear before Him. As it encourages the faithful to be strong against the temptations of the devil, Sacred Scripture expresses this truth very powerfully in 1 Peter 5:10: "And after you have suffered a little while, the God of all grace, who has called you to his eternal glory in Christ, will himself restore, establish, and strengthen you." And St. Paul writes: "he who began a good work in you will bring it to completion at the day of Jesus Christ" (Phil 1:6).

We should pray particularly for persons who are nearing death and ask God in His mercy to grant them the grace of final perseverance. With this grace, they will be able to die in a state of soul that is pleasing to God and therefore be open to obtaining eternal life, though they may have to go through a phase of final purification in purgatory. The main object of our prayer is that they die in a state of sanctifying grace, which is already a participation in God's own life. Heaven is obviously the next step.

But what about the physical care for such people? Apart from medical treatments, the Church teaches that in very painful illnesses, morphine and other drugs can be administered to patients in order to relieve suffering, even if it means a shortening of his or her life. There is nothing wrong with this; it is an act of charity, and it may relieve the person from the temptation to despair.

But we must also remember that not all pain is bad; it can also have a positive effect. Pain is an opportunity for the suffering person to make atonement for her sins and to offer it for the good of others. Pain born courageously, even heroically, can purge a person from attachment to sin, reduce the suffering in purgatory, and prepare her for eternal life. It can be truly redemptive in the final months or days of a person's life because it gives them the chance to unite themselves with Christ on the Cross, who is the cause of all salvation.

At times, people can go overboard in their efforts to remove all pain for those who are suffering or dying. It can even lead to the deliberate taking of a life simply to end their pain or anxiety; certain forms of hospice care can even become a cover for euthanasia, which will always be a grave sin, whether it is done with or without the permission of the sufferer. One can never take an innocent human life.

Though no one can be sure of the grace of final perseverance outside of a special revelation from God,[4] we do have the assurance that if a person has sincerely striven to lead a

---

[4] See Council of Trent, session 7, can. 16.

good Christian life, is sorry for his sins, and received the sacraments faithfully, particularly Anointing of the Sick, God will grant him the grace to be with Him forever in heaven.

But we cannot assume this grace, and out of love for the person, especially for one who seems to have been far from God during his life or at the moment of death, we must do all we can to assist him or her. To pray and sacrifice for a person who is dying or close to death is, therefore, one of the greatest acts of charity that we can do on earth. And of course, all efforts to make life pleasant for this person in his final days, to bring him a certain joy and companionship, and above all, to inspire and encourage him, is to pave the way directly for his passage to the life without end.

The most important step is, of course, to arrange that a priest come to him, to hear his confession and to anoint him. Anointing of the Sick is a direct preparation for death. It gives a special grace to the person to avoid the temptation to despair and to make many acts of hope in God's love and mercy. Holy Communion, called Viaticum, is a very powerful help for the person's last journey since Christ Himself comes to assist him with His Body, Blood, Soul, and Divinity. It is also very helpful if the priest can impart the Apostolic Pardon, which can remit all temporal punishment due to sin if the person has the right dispositions. If a person is wearing the scapular of Our Lady of Mount Carmel, we can encourage him or her to make many acts of personal entrusting to her motherly care, and we can pray for her special intercession for them on the Saturday after their death.

In addition to anointing and Holy Communion, it is of great help to say the Rosary with the dying person and perhaps whisper in his ear many aspirations that he can repeat such as "Jesus, I love you"; "Jesus, Mary, and Joseph, I give you my heart and my soul"; "Most Sacred Heart of Jesus, have mercy" or other prayers to the angels and saints. (Medical doctors have affirmed that even patients in a coma can hear what people are saying around them.) There are many beautiful and uplifting prayers in good manuals of Catholic devotion we can use to assist the dying individual. These prayers have the effect of elevating the person's mind and heart so that he can confidently and lovingly await his coming encounter with God.

The ideal is that all of the above will be done by family members or close relatives who also remain physically close to the dying person. Or they may be done by the person's close friend or friends. The death of a relative or friend is often an excellent moment to give witness to other family members or friends about the meaning of life and God's existence. In many cases, they can actually be moved to conversion or to making a good confession as they witness people of faith taking good care of the ailing person and giving him or her their loving attention.

Whatever the circumstances, it is safe to affirm that helping a person to die well and in the state of grace is one of the greatest acts of co-redemption, if not the greatest, that we can perform for a person on earth. At those moments, we are the instruments of Christ's saving grace, which can enter and transform a person when he or she needs it the most.

CHAPTER 14

Easter Joy

"Thomas answered him, 'My Lord and my God!'" (John 20:28)

WE CAN IMAGINE THE JOY AND HOPE that Thomas experienced when he finally believed. The other disciples had seen Christ on the afternoon of the Resurrection, but for some reason Thomas was not with them. Perhaps he was too discouraged or afraid to return to the upper room where Christ had celebrated the Passover. Perhaps he was simply distracted, trying to figure it all out, and needed space, so to speak. But whatever the reason, his doubts disappeared when he saw the risen Christ. It was not a hallucination. It was not some wild tale invented by the holy women and his fellow Apostles. It was the true Christ, body and soul, yet risen and glorious, who invited Thomas to put his finger and hand into His hand and side.

Easter is the greatest event in human history, when Jesus, both God and man, rose from the sepulcher by His own power. He who had suffered in such a painful and tragic way triumphed over death, and because of His triumph we, too, shall triumph over death one day. This is the perennial message of Christianity, and it is at the heart of the Good News that people must keep hearing. It is the vital force behind our redemption, for through the power of the risen

Christ, we shall rise from the dead ourselves, even though all that is left of our bodies may be a bit of bone or dust. No wonder the first believers called Easter Sunday the eighth day, or the day of the New Creation.

Where there was death—and a most bloody and painful death—there is now everlasting life. Where there was no hope, there is now the greatest hope. Where there was only tragedy or meaninglessness, there is now the greatest meaning and purpose. Human life is not absurd or pointless. Not even the greatest suffering or despair can conquer human beings as long as they believe in the one who conquered the greatest suffering and despair.

"I will see you again and your hearts will rejoice, and no one will take your joy from you" (John 16:22). Earthly pleasures come and go. Even the happiest human events often have some bitterness or ugliness about them because of sin. But the joy of God's grace, through Christ's Resurrection, is permanent. If we don't reject that joy by grave sin, it will always be within as a spiritual reality and as a promise of glory. It is very much related to our divine filiation whereby we are brothers and sisters of Christ and members of His family. This is what gives a Christian indomitable joy and cheerfulness despite the sorrows and ambiguities of this life. It also gives us the hope of a future life with God and His angels in paradise, a hope that nothing can take away, as the Lord Himself told His Apostles. It is that permanent and powerful spirit of victory that is behind the Alleluia of Easter. It is also in the soul of all of those who believe in and love Christ above all things.

At times, we can have a very superficial view of joy. We can easily confuse it with pleasure or just having fun. That pleasure could be a movie we like, a sport we play, games on the computer, or simply a time with good friends of ours with a lot of jokes and kidding around. Of course there is nothing wrong with these things; in some way they are even anticipations on this earth of the everlasting happiness of heaven. But real Christian joy has a deeper source. It is based on the supernatural virtue of hope, which was infused into our souls at Baptism and with God's grace will grow throughout our life. This hope endures beyond all human desires and ambitions, which come and go with time. But the hope that Christ gives is based on His Paschal Mystery: that marvelous union of suffering and victory that overcomes all sadness.

If we are to be true co-redeemers, we should be experiencing that supernatural joy and hope always. We may have many sorrows in life, but we should not give in to sadness. We can even feel the temptation to become discouraged or to despair at different events in our life, but with supernatural hope and joy we can turn those feelings and temptations into victory, like turning a minus into a plus in mathematics. The only difference between a minus and a plus is one vertical line, the line that leads upward. That vertical line is our faith and hope in the God who loves us and the Redeemer who saved us and sent us His Holy Spirit. With this kind of attitude, we are truly in a "win-win situation." As St. Paul put it, "We know that in everything God works for good with those who love him" (Rom 8:28). This is not some kind of naïve optimism but a reality that is based on the knowledge of God's saving grace in our lives, despite our weakness.

The Spirit Who Gives Laughter

A good friend of mine once said that, in his opinion, the Holy Spirit is the divine Person who gives laughter to people. Certainly, the great theologians of the past have distinguished joy as one of His fruits in a soul, along with others such as peace and kindness. Since He proceeds from the love of the Father and the Son and is often called the Spirit of Love, we can see how that is true. Joy comes from the deep conviction that we are loved and that even our sufferings have a purpose. Such is the profound work of the Holy Spirit, who in many ways is the unseen hero of our spiritual lives. He is the One who gives us the inner conviction that we are children of God; He is the One who can turn suffering into victory; He is the One who, little by little, converts us into Christ—so that we, too, can redeem the world in union with Him. He was the One who came upon the disciples at Pentecost with His marvelous gifts and fruits and gave them such confidence and power. He also gave them the magnificent gift of joy.

Freedom from Three Prisons

In many ways St. Paul is the apostle of joy. Not only does he speak continually about having faith in Christ and the greatness of His Mystical Body on earth in his letters but he speaks about the Christians' victory in the end. You can detect the Holy Spirit working inside him when he wrote these stirring words: "For you did not receive the spirit of slavery to fall back into fear, but you have received the spirit of sonship. When we cry, 'Abba! Father!' it is the Spirit himself bearing witness with our spirit that we are children of God" (Rom 8:15–16).

This is truly the heart of Christianity's redemptive message. A baptized Christian is a joyful and liberated individual. She is a winner, in the full sense of the world. She is no longer in the prison of materialism, which not only afflicted the ancient world but now our own post-modern world. Materialism is indeed a prison because it confines our freedom and makes us think that we are mere animals, subject to the most pleasing stimuli, which we must necessarily follow, whether it be money, food, or sexual pleasure. It ultimately denies that men and women were created in the image and likeness of God—that they are free and have immortal souls. Materialism denies the greatness of a life of virtue, and, quite frankly, it produces only boredom in the end: boredom with oneself, boredom with others, boredom with the world in general. This is what Pope Francis emphasized with young men and women at the 2016 World Youth Day in Krakow, as we mentioned in the Preface of this book: "Jesus is not the Lord of comfort, security, and ease. Following Jesus demands a good dose of courage, a readiness to trade in the sofa for a pair of walking shoes and to set out on new and uncharted paths."[1]

Christ's life and Resurrection are the most wonderful and exciting events in human history. They also liberate us from two of our greatest enemies: ignorance and despair. Ignorance of God and the soul is a terrible affliction for

---

[1] Pope Francis, "Address of the Holy Father" (World Youth Day, Prayer Vigil with the Young People, Campus Misericordiae, Kraków, July 30, 2016).

people. They may be very knowledgeable in some matters, they may be honor students, they may be tenured professors—but if they don't know the purpose of human existence, they're in a very sad condition. I remember once seeing a Calvin and Hobbes (a humorous series of cartoons about a little boy and his toy tiger that were popular some years ago) scenario where Calvin, who is the class rebel, raises his hand to ask a question. The teacher is delighted that at last the boy is showing some interest in her subject, and calls upon him. "What is the point of human existence?" he asks. The teacher, visibly upset, answers: "I meant any questions about the subject at hand." To which the mischievous boy answers, "Frankly, I'd like the have the issue resolved before I expend any more energy on this."[2]

Well put. Ignorance of what really matters is like a dark tunnel that encloses many people today. There is a lot of information on computers, instantly available and now multiplied in gigabytes, but can a person find any permanent lesson or truth in it all about what is really important? Truth most often comes with calm study and reflection, connecting important facts with essential conclusions. And the greatest truths come only from faith, namely those concerning human nature and our ultimate destiny. Christ's redemption and His Church give us those ultimate essential answers without which we can never be happy. A world in which there is no right or wrong is a chaotic and violent world. We see it every day. Such a world can only lead to dictatorship—not only political dictatorship but also what

---

[2] Bill Watterson, "Calvin and Hobbes," March 6, 2012, https://www. gocomics.com/calvinandhobbes/2012/03/06/.

Pope Benedict XVI called the "dictatorship of relativism."[3] This mindset holds sway over much of the Western world today and prevents people from taking a clear moral stand on any situation since everything, even God, is opinionable. Not the least of its effects is that relativism takes out the challenge and adventure of human life. Like materialism, it is very *boring* because it gives us nothing to live for, to fight for, or to die for.

Besides materialism and ignorance, Christ has liberated us from still another prison: that of pessimism and self-pity. This state of mind is really the consequence of the first two prisons sin creates in us. It is a kind of sadness and hopelessness about others and about the future. It is related to egotism, which encloses us within the narrow purview of our own mind and feelings. With no outlet beyond ourselves, we lose hope. To use a thought coined by ancient skeptics and quoted by Pope Benedict XVI in his second encyclical: *De nihilo in nihil incedimus*, "How quickly we fall back from nothingness into nothingness."[4] Self-pity and pessimism can be truly paralyzing not only for our own lives but also for those around us. We can see it in many people's negative attitudes about society, the Church, and people in general. But the person who really believes and lives the mystery of co-redemption is like a light in the world's dark tunnel and a breath of freedom into the prisons that trap people's minds and hearts.

---

[3] Joseph Ratzinger, "Homily of His Eminence Card. Joseph Ratzinger, Dean of the College of Cardinals" (Vatican Basilica, April 18, 2005).

[4] Pope Benedict XVI, *Spe Salvi*, §2.

Perpetual Youthfulness

"I am the way, and the truth, and the life; no one comes to the Father, but by me" (John 14:6). We need to be convinced that Christ's Paschal Mystery can truly work within us. We must believe that we can be people of greater prayer and contemplation; that we can have more charity and kindness in dealing with others; that we can live chastity well in thought, desire, and action; that we can be apostles and bring others closer to God. The last words that Jesus spoke to His Apostles were words of encouragement in the real meaning of that word, which is to *give courage*. "All authority in heaven and on earth has been given to me. . . . and behold, I am with you always, to the close of the age" (Matt 28:18, 20). Only ten days after He ascended into heaven, He sent the Third Person of the Blessed Trinity—the Great Consoler and the Great Motivator, the Living Breath of God's love—into the souls of His Apostles in Jerusalem. They saw things much more clearly with the help of this divine Person, and received the impetus and courage to go forth and to bear witness to all that they had heard from Christ. They were filled with His gifts, as we said above, and their joy and hope were multiplied in a supernatural way, far beyond what they could experience on their own. If they had been afraid because of the Roman or Jewish authorities, they now received a grace that impelled them to take tremendous risks for Christ and to build up His Church on earth.

At the passing of Pope John Paul II thousands of young people were gathered in St. Peter's Square, accompanying the Pontiff as his life slowly ebbed away in his upstairs room. There was a quiet expectation of the inevitable and much prayer. At one point, the Pope was escorted to the window where he could see the immense multitude of young people praying for him. He could barely speak, but one of his attendants could hear him gasp the following: "I have all my life been looking for you, and now you have come to me." After John Paul II went to God, Pope Benedict XVI stated that he could see the perennial youthfulness of the Church during those days—not only because of the youth of most people there but because of the spirit of hope that could be seen and felt. "Yes, the Church is alive," he said in his 2005 inaugural homily. "This is the wonderful experience of these days . . . And the Church is young. She holds within herself the future of the world and therefore shows each of us the way towards the future."[5] Later on, in his gathering with youths in Australia, he used the word *transform*—a term that he employed a lot and that has a definite resonance of early Christianity about it: "To be truly alive is to be transformed from within, open to the energy of God's love. In accepting the power of the Holy Spirit, you can also transform your families, communities, and nations. Set free the gifts!"[6]

As co-redeemers, each in our own way, we should be willing to take risks for Christ and His Church. The Holy Spirit transformed a group of fearful, doubting men into a virtual army for Christ on earth two thousand years ago. If we stay close to the Holy Spirit, He will bring us His

---

[5] Pope Benedict XVI, "Homily of His Holiness Benedict XVI" (Mass, Imposition of the Pallium, and Conferral of the Fisherman's Ring for the Beginning of the Petrine Ministry of the Bishop of Rome, St. Peter's Square, April 24, 2005).

[6] Pope Benedict XVI, "Address of His Holiness," (World Youth Day Vigil, July, 2008).

marvelous gifts and give us a contagious joy and hope the poor sad earth cannot resist. "When you send forth your Spirit, they are created; and you renew the face of the earth" (Psalm 104:30).

CHAPTER 15

Mary Co-Redemptrix

"Behold, I am the handmaid of the Lord; let it be to me according to your word." (Luke 1:38)

IN THE COURSE OF THIS LITTLE BOOK, we have considered different redemptive actions: prayer, sacrifice, charity, joy, faith. Each of them has a unique way of bringing about man's salvation and bringing Christ's kingdom to those around us. Indeed, throughout history the great saints have literally "saved the world" by performing these actions, often to the point of heroism.

One thinks of St. Justin Martyr back in the second century, who pointed the way with his mind, and with his blood, to Christ the *Logos* or Word, who fulfilled the highest aspirations of philosophy. One thinks of St. Benedict, whose monastic foundations and spiritual example sanctified a great part of Europe for many centuries. One thinks of St. Catherine of Siena, whose insistent prayer and sacrifice brought the pope back to Rome in the fourteenth century. One thinks of St. Thérèse of Lisieux, who lived her "little way" so exquisitely and was an inspiration for millions to find God in small, everyday things.

Saint Joseph, spouse of Mary and Head of the Holy Family, had a most special role to play in our redemption. To all intents and purposes, he was the father of Jesus, and as a father he not only gave him his name and lineage but his profession. Only in Heaven will we know how much he influenced his son: in the way he spoke, how he worked, his manner of dealing with everyday things. As we said in the chapter on Matrimony, he is also the model for all Christian fathers in their dedication and protection of their families.

But there was one human person who surpassed them all, who was filled with grace from the moment of her conception. Every moment of her life was like a hosanna of praise to God. Though she did no miracles while living on earth as future saints would do, she brought the greatest miracle to the world—her Son and Redeemer. As Pope Francis stated in his homily of January 1, 2020: "Mary will forever be the Mother of God. She is both woman and mother: this is what is essential. From her, a woman, salvation came forth and thus there is no salvation without a woman."[1] Her cooperation with God was complete and wholehearted. As we have seen throughout this book, such a generous cooperation is necessary for bringing grace and life to the world.

For this reason, Mary may be called *Co-Redemptrix* in the most powerful meaning of the word. Always keeping in mind her complete union with Christ, the Sole Redeemer, as the Pope clarified in his December 12, 2019 homily.[2] Her whole life was centered upon Him, from His conception to His Resurrection. We can only imagine the joy and expectation in her heart as she awaited His birth. We get a glimpse of it in her words to her cousin Elizabeth: "My soul magnifies

---

[1] Pope Francis, "Homily of his Holiness Pope Francis" (Holy Mass on the Solemnity of Mary, Mother of God, 53rd World Day of Peace, Vatican Basilica, January 1, 2020).

[2] See Introduction.

the Lord, and my spirit rejoices in God my Savior" (Luke 1:46). And after Jesus was born, she continued to reflect, give thanks, and pray. She didn't let things pass by her superficially but "pondered them in her heart," as St. Luke tells us in his Gospel (Luke 2:19). We said before that prayer is essential for salvation, along with faith. She shows us the way to both. She, with the help of the Holy Spirit, was able to see God working in history and the part that she and others had to play. Such is the essence of co-redemption at any time or place.

As a Loving Mother with Her Child

Everything that Mary did on earth was to further her Son's redemptive mission. This is beautifully described in Chapter 8 of the Dogmatic Constitution *Lumen Gentium*:

> Thus Mary, a daughter of Adam, consenting to the divine Word, became the mother of Jesus, the one and only Mediator. Embracing God's salvific will with a full heart and impeded by no sin, she devoted herself totally as a handmaid of the Lord to the Person and work of her Son, *under Him and with Him*, by the grace of Almighty God, serving the mystery of redemption. Rightly therefore the holy Fathers see her as used by God not merely in a passive way, but as freely cooperating in the work of human salvation through faith and obedience.[3]

---

[3] Second Vatican Council, Dogmatic Constitution on the Church *Lumen Gentium* (November 21, 1964), §56, emphasis added.

I italicized the phrase "under Him and with Him" (in Latin, *sub Ipso et cum Ipso*) because it is essential for understanding her role.[4] As a human person, she is under her Son, who is Christ the Son of God, since she owes her own salvation to Him; while at the same time, as His mother and ours, she works with her Son continually for the salvation of all mankind. We could even say that, as His mother, she is "over" her Son in a certain way because He will fulfill her every request, as He did at the miracle of Cana.

From the words of Scripture and the Tradition of the Church, we know very well the ways in which she cooperated with God's saving plan. After accepting her role as His mother, she carried Jesus in her womb then raised and educated Him with Joseph, her spouse. As all good mothers do, she must have taught Him His first prayers and helped Him take His first steps. Her life and Joseph's were certainly made up of ordinary things, but these ordinary things also make up the very core of redemptive work. "For by His incarnation the Son of God has united Himself in some fashion with every man. He worked with human hands, He thought with a human mind, acted by human choice and loved with a human heart. Born of the Virgin Mary, He has truly been made one of us, like us in all things except sin."[5]

It was her hands and words that first taught the Christ child how to walk and how to speak. At the beginning of

---

4   Second Vatican Council, *Lumen Gentium*, §56. See the original Latin text: "Ita Maria filia Adam . . . semetipsam ut Domini ancillam personae et operi Filii sui totaliter devovit, sub Ipso et cum Ipso, omnipotentis Dei gratia, mysterii redemptionis inserviens."

5   Second Vatican Council, *Gaudium et Spes*, §22.

Jesus's public life, Mary was the first one to invite her Son to do a miracle. The miracles would be necessary to convince others, including the Apostles, that He was truly the Messiah and Redeemer. As we said above, it was Mary who set the stage for Him to show His divine power, even "before His time." As a result of that miracle, redemption manifested itself publicly, so to speak. As St. John records, "This, the first of his signs, Jesus did at Cana in Galilee, and manifested his glory; and his disciples believed in him" (John 2:11).

During His public years, as He formed His Apostles and gathered many people around Him through His words and miracles, Mary remained in the background. She did not thrust herself into the public eye in order to receive praise for being the mother of Jesus. Perhaps she remained at home, working prayerfully and silently; by this time, it appears that Joseph her spouse had died. She may have joined the group of holy women who ministered to Christ and His Apostles. But if she did so, she blended in perfectly with the others and passed unnoticed. Again, even though her role in our redemption is profound and irreplaceable, she remained hidden, as she did from the beginning.

Her greatest co-redemptive work was at the Crucifixion. There she must have suffered a sorrow that is impossible for us to express in words.

As Pope Francis put it, speaking of Mary's suffering at Calvary: "Here Mary is united to the Son in the martyrdom of her heart and in the offering of His life for the salvation of humanity. Our Lady shared in the pain of the Son and accepted with Him the will of the Father, in that obedience that bears fruit, that grants the true victory over evil and death."[6] If you can imagine what a mother would go through seeing her own flesh and blood being crucified before her, you can begin to feel her suffering. And if you add to that her knowledge of who her Son was and what He was trying to do—the anguish is indescribable. She who never committed a sin offered her life in union with her Son for the sins of the world. Yet the Gospel, the inspired word of God, simply says she was "standing by the Cross" (in Latin, *stabat mater juxta Crucem*) (John 19:25). She did not faint, nor cry out hysterically, nor give in to despair—but just *stood there*, and co-redeemed. In other words, she simply did what she had to do: to be with her Son, supporting Him at this central moment of our redemption, when He was conquering sin and the devil and saving the entire human race.

Pope St. John Paul II, in his encyclical *Redemptoris Mater,* tried to capture Our Lady's anguish in some way by contrasting what she had heard at the beginning from the angel at the Annunciation—that her Son would be great, that His kingdom would endure forever—with what was happening on Calvary. In John Paul II's words, she was experiencing the very "negation of those words" of joy and hope, yet she continued to stand firmly in support of what her Son had to do.[7] "How great, how heroic then is the obedience of faith shown by Mary in the face of God's unsearchable judgments! How completely she abandons herself to God without reserve."[8]

---

[6] Pope Francis, "General Audience" (St. Peter's Square, October 23, 2013).

[7] Pope St. John Paul II, Encyclical Letter on the Blessed Virgin Mary in the Life of the Pilgrim Church *Redemptoris Mater* (March 25, 1987), §18.

[8] Pope St. John Paul II, *Redemptoris Mater*, §18.

How She Continues to Serve Us

Certainly, the Virgin Mary's fortitude can help us in moments of great sorrow or trial, when it's hard to fathom or to accomplish the will of God.

It could be an illness, a serious misunderstanding, or a tragic death in the family. Let's learn to go to her often, perhaps like a small child who needs to go to his mother for strength when he's hurt himself, when he's too weak to do his work, or even to pray. We can be confident that, in uniting ourselves to the Mother of Christ in those moments, we, too, can bring grace to the world, and like that small boy dying of cancer mentioned before, we can offer ourselves as a holocaust for the love of God and others.

The co-redemptive response to ordinary sufferings and worse is to put them into the wounds of Christ crucified.[9] This is what Mary did when she took all the pain of sin and mockery on Calvary into herself, with her Son, and made the human race "right" again with God. At that very moment, she became the New Eve, taking away the sinful stain on the human race left by the first Eve. Somehow, you and I in our own sufferings, very small compared to hers, can unite ourselves with her and her Son—and bring redemptive grace to the world.

Even after the Crucifixion and Resurrection, she continued to serve her Son and the Church. She gave strength to the Apostles after the Ascension as she was praying with them (see Acts 1:14). The Apostles must have felt like orphans, fearful before the tremendous mission that Christ

---

[9] Escrivá, *The Way*, no. 288.

had set before them—but they received confidence and consolation from His mother. They knew that her presence and her prayer were very powerful before God. She was praying with them for the coming of the Holy Spirit, who would give them the truth, grace, and courage that they would need to go forth and to conquer the world for Christ.

Her powerful co-redemptive role continues in the Church throughout the centuries. Her chief interest is to bring her Son and His kingdom to people's souls and lives. We cannot think that her motherly heart extends to Catholics only. In addition to extending to all human beings, it extends in a particular way to all Christians united by Baptism who have a common faith in Christ the Redeemer. Mary's intercession, we know, takes away nothing from Christ's power; it actually demonstrates her Son's divine power and goodness as He shares His redemptive grace with her and with all Christians for the salvation of the world. This divine goodness is the source of all co-redemption, first in Mary His mother, and then in the lives of ordinary Christians in the midst of the world. Such a conviction, in my opinion, should empower even more the evangelical zeal of all Christians; they have a special grace to bring the truth and grace of the Redeemer to all the circumstances of their lives, as the first disciples did.

As we near the end of this book, let us ask her to intercede for all believers in Christ. All mothers want their children to be united; they do not want disagreements and quarrels among them. We can be sure that she is interceding for all Christians to be once again united in the Body of her Son, the one true Church, despite many centuries of controversy and division. Belief in her love and intercession will always pave the way for more understanding and reconciliation among the followers of Jesus Christ. In the words of Pope St. John Paul II, "Mary belongs indissolubly to the mystery of Christ, and she belongs also to the mystery of the Church from the beginning, from the day of the Church's birth ... It is precisely Mary's faith which marks the beginning of the new and eternal Covenant of God with man in Jesus Christ: this heroic faith of hers 'precedes' the apostolic witness of the Church and ever remains in the Church's heart, hidden like a special heritage of God's revelation."[10]

The Mystery of Co-Redemption: She and You

The mystery of co-redemption ... and you. This is one more way to entitle this little book. Perhaps we could finish it by saying *the mystery of co-redemption ... and she.* Devotion to Mary will lead us to even greater devotion to Christ, for Mary never keeps the honor and veneration for herself but gives them to her Son. As we said in the Introduction, Pope Francis has commented that Mary in her simplicity and humility would not want to be called Co-Redemptrix, if such a title existed in her lifetime. She considered herself to be simply the handmaid of God and one more disciple of her Son; her whole life was to serve and to pass unnoticed.

This is very good advice for ourselves as well as we end this book. All of us simply want to be faithful disciples of Christ, who is the only Redeemer. If we can somehow bring salvation to others through Him and with Him, we are happy to do so, even without having the title of co-redeemers.

---

[10] Pope St. John Paul II, *Redemptoris Mater*, §27.

By being close to Mary, we can bring Christ to the world, for we will "incarnate" Him as we pray, work, love, and suffer for Him in ways similar to Mary. Besides small prayers and personal aspirations that we can direct to her, an excellent devotion is to contemplate and pray the Rosary frequently. Each of the mysteries, including the Mysteries of Light (Luminous Mysteries) established by Pope St. John Paul II, can draw us more completely into her life and the life of her Son. The Annunciation, the Birth in Bethlehem, the Crucifixion, the Resurrection—each mystery has its own message and power to sanctify and transform. Speaking of us all, the mysteries of the Rosary are living models and exemplars of how we should be living and how we should treat other people. If we contemplate them and pray them consistently, our own existence will become more and more redemptive as we enter more and more personally into the existence of Jesus and Mary.

Finally, how can we forget the glorious completion of Mary's life on earth? "The Immaculate Mother of God, the ever Virgin Mary, having completed the course of her earthly life, was assumed body and soul into heavenly glory."[11] Mary represents for us, along with Christ, the final glorified condition of the human race. We know that the mystery of redemption will be fulfilled, and we hope that someday we, too, will be united forever with God and that our glorified bodies will be reunited with our souls. We will then see the Lord face-to-face, and our joy can never be taken from us. The ultimate result of Christ's redemption is

---

[11] Pope Ven. Pius XII, Apostolic Constitution Defining the Dogma of the Assumption *Munificentissimus Deus* (November 1, 1950), §44.

the new heaven and the new earth, where Mary shall reign as queen.

It is to that kingdom that we are bound. It is to that kingdom that Christ's redemptive work is calling us and which we, His disciples on earth, are trying to build. Through Mary's intercession, we hope to join her and her Son, both in body and soul: not with a body stained by sin and death but with a glorified body that will live forever in God.

"Behold, I make all things new" (Rev 21:5). The last book of Scripture proclaims the triumphant words of the Lamb who is Christ, who will take possession of the entire universe when He comes again. Such is the goal of our life as well; in union with the redemptive sacrifice of Christ and with Mary His mother, we want to make all things *new*.